America's Silent
Investigators

America's Silent Investigators

☆ THE STORY OF THE POSTAL
  INSPECTORS WHO PROTECT
  THE UNITED STATES MAIL

By Elinore Denniston

DODD, MEAD & COMPANY, NEW YORK

Printed in the United States of America
by Vail-Ballou Press, Inc., Binghamton, N. Y.

For the nice children of Mike Chicoris:
Elaine, Michael, Gregory, Andrew

Contents

CONCLUSION

INTRODUCTION

I ☆ Introducing
the Postal Inspectors

LET'S TAKE a brief look at the American postal system. Few of us ever give much thought to it. We stamp a letter, drop it in a box and—that's that.

And yet this great institution, whose workings we know so little about, is closer to us than any other branch of the government. We watch the mailman plodding on his way—the mailman who, as we will discover, knows us better than does any other government employee. We use the mails daily for business or friendship, and one of our first comments on coming home is, "Are there any letters? What was in the mail today?"

More Americans visit post offices than visit movie theaters or ball games. How many of us are aware that the United States postal system is the largest communications organization in the entire world? Indeed, it is the world's biggest business.

How is this possible? Well, through postal savings it handles one of the world's biggest banks. Because of the number of buildings it owns or rents for post offices, it is

11

one of the biggest real estate companies, with over 45,000 postal installations, including branches, stations, and so forth. It controls the largest fleet of trucks and cars in America, about 100,000 vehicles. It employs over half a million people, of whom 200,000 are mail carriers.

In a single day more mail is distributed in New York City than in all of Canada, while Americans send and receive two-thirds of the entire world's mail, delivered over 2,500,000 miles of routes. Of the more than 70,000,000,-000 pieces of mail it handles yearly, only fifteen pieces out of every million are lost or stolen.

This seems incredible when we remember through how many hands the mail must pass and the many ways in which it may be delivered. A letter may be sent by any one of a number of methods, or by a combination of them, depending on where it has to go: by train or truck, by carriers who deliver on foot with mail sacks on their backs, by car or truck, by ship or airplane, by horseback and—until recently —by dog sled.

Whatever the method of delivery required, the privacy of sender and receiver is protected. When you put a five-cent stamp on a letter and drop it down a mail chute, there is not a single person, not even the Postmaster General, who may open that letter. This law applies even when the letter is suspected of containing evidence as to the whereabouts of a wanted criminal.

The Constitution of the United States guarantees you absolute privacy from the time the letter is mailed until it is received by the person to whom it is addressed. This guarantee was granted by a Supreme Court decision written by Justice Field:

"Letters and sealed packages . . . in the mails are as fully guaranteed from examination and inspection, except in their outward form and weight, as if they were retained by the parties forwarding them in their own domiciles. The Constitutional guarantee of the people to be secure in their papers against unreasonable searches and seizures extended to their papers, thus closed against inspection, wherever they may be . . . No law of Congress can place in the hands of officers connected with the postal service any authority to invade the secrecy of letters, and such sealed packages in the mail; and all regulations adopted as to mail matter of this kind must be in subordination to the general principle embodied in the Fourth Amendment to the Constitution."

The only exceptions to this law are dead letters, which may be opened by clerks in the dead-letter branches, to try to find the address of the sender, or unusual situations in time of war when the security of the country is at stake.

There have been many times when detectives investigating a crime have discovered to their surprise that they are not permitted to open a letter that might furnish the very evidence they are seeking.

This same respect for individual privacy is protected by the United States Postal Service in other ways. Postmasters may not give out the names of box holders or furnish information about money orders they have issued or cashed.

All this, however—the delivery of the mail and the protection of individual privacy—is only one element in the complicated working of the postal system. The operation of all post offices must be regularly checked to see that the books balance, that the post-office property and stamps—

twenty-eight billion stamps a year—are accounted for, that the service is efficient, and to arrange for the renting or purchase of new property.

Another job is the protection of the integrity of the mails, to see that the public is guarded against fraud of many kinds and from the dangerous small group that, unfortunately, cannot be entirely rooted out of any country, those people who make use of the mails for criminal purposes. This may entail anything from shadowing train robbers to rendering a bomb harmless; from exposing medical and business frauds to preventing the diversion of American dollars into the hands of the Communists; from cleaning out the Black Hand in Chicago to tracking down mail thieves on a pursuit that may extend halfway around the world; from exposing and prosecuting the people who distribute obscene matter in letters, books and magazines through the mails to stopping at the source the distribution of Communist propaganda sent by mail. These two latter activities receive comparatively little publicity except when the distributor of obscene material is caught and prosecuted, but it is a silent warfare that is constantly being waged for the public welfare.

The protection of the world's largest mail is handled by a group of one thousand men, the American Postal Inspectors, who constitute the oldest law-enforcement organization in America. They are probably the finest federal investigative agency in the United States; and, indeed, it seems likely that they may well be the finest anywhere in the world today.

How odd it is that we Americans often quote the well-known statement about the Canadian Mounted Police, "The Mountie always gets his man," and yet our own Postal

Inspectors have a more spectacular record. That record of convictions, in cases brought to trial, ranges from a low of 97.5 to a high of 99.1, unparalleled anywhere. In the proud history of the Postal Inspectors only one man has ever proved to be false to his trust.

"But why," people sometimes ask, "do we know so little about these remarkable men to whom we owe so much?"

One answer to that lies in the name by which they have come to be known, "America's Silent Investigators." They do not seek personal publicity. They do not even desire credit for their great achievements. It is neither praise nor reward for which they work, it is the integrity of the postal system.

Sometimes people become rather cynical about their public servants. When they do, it is as well for them to remember the loyal and self-effacing group of men who, day and night, employ their wits and their ingenuity, their energy and their hard training, to see that the United States mail is protected from theft and fraud. Though their salaries are fixed and they do not become rich, these men save the American public millions of dollars a year; and, by exposing and punishing fraud, they prevent gullible people from wasting enormous sums of money on all sorts of fake claims.

While people in more and more fields tend to work in groups, the Postal Inspectors often proceed as individuals, each man determining for himself what cases he will work on, how and when he will handle them, and assuming full responsibility for the results. Over the years they have become one of the most flexible and efficient groups of detectives anywhere, called upon by investigative groups in other government departments for assistance or, at times, even by other governments.

And here is the most extraordinary fact of all: the cost of the investigative arm of the post office is one of the lowest of any federal investigative group, except for some very small organizations, in spite of the fact that its record is the highest. On top of that the Postal Inspectors return at least half a million dollars to the public every year, which they have recovered from robbery, forgery, or mail theft.

It is these men about whom this book is written. It is men like them, unknown, too often unthanked, who help to keep America safe and free and to protect the privacy of the individual citizen.

Of course, the highly skilled group whom we call America's Silent Investigators did not come about by accident or all at once. It took many years to create the postal system as it exists today. In fact, for a long time after the colonies were settled, there was no postal system at all.

Ship captains simply dumped what mail they had brought from England on a table at some convenient coffeehouse near the port, and there it stayed until the colonists came along to pick up their own letters and those of their neighbors. People who farmed outside the small coastal towns might not receive their mail for many weeks, and the risk of loss or theft was extremely large. After all, no one was responsible for what happened.

But the colonies began to grow in size; business was expanding; communications had to be established and stabilized. Something had to be done about the mails. And so began, slow step by slow step, the laborious process of trial and error that was to create eventually the Postal System as we know it today.

Part I ☆ THE PAST

II ☆ The Way It Started

As THE COLONISTS began to cultivate farms farther and farther away from the seaports and towns, it was no longer possible for them to go on board the newly arrived ship to collect their mail. Nor was it satisfactory to trust that a letter, often long awaited and of vital importance, or at any rate containing news about a family who had not been heard of for many months, would be passed on from hand to hand until, more by good luck than good management, it reached the person for whom it was intended.

Aside from the length of time it took a letter to reach its destination and the frequency of loss, there was another problem. Since there was no one legally accountable for the mail, and no law, anyhow, to protect privacy, there was nothing to prevent people from opening letters that were not addressed to them and picking up private information that might be to their advantage. Unscrupulous businessmen found out what customers their competitors had and what prices they charged for their products. Gossips could learn about the personal affairs of their friends and neighbors.

Massachusetts was the first colony to try to do something

19

to protect the mail and bring about some order. In 1639 the Massachusetts General Court appointed an official place for all mail to be distributed. This was the house of one Richard Fairbanks who, because he was to be held responsible for the safety of the mail in his care, was to receive two pennies for every letter he handled.

The next major step came in 1672 when New York started a regular post to Boston. Up to that time the colonies had remained, on the whole, separate entities with little communication among them. There wasn't much of a path to follow. In fact, it was up to the postrider to seek out the best route and then blaze it so that other travelers could follow it. That Boston Post Road still exists, one of the first of the country's highways. Indeed, many of our first highways were "post" roads, trails blazed by men on horseback carrying the mail, or the post as it was then called by the colonists.

This system was a vast improvement for the colonists who, before men began regularly "riding post," had to forward their letters in any way they could, sometimes handing them to travelers who were going in the right direction or, if they could afford it, sending them by private messenger.

Little by little a crude postal system was set up, as each colony tried to cope with the problems of distributing the mail within its own boundaries or, more difficult, in establishing some kind of regular communications between one colony and another. The system was haphazard and inefficient and it cost the British government considerably more than it ever received from it. This was a great disappointment to the British, because one of the primary reasons for Parliament passing a Post Office Act in 1710, which included her colonies, was to help pay for the War of the Spanish Succession, which it had engineered in order to maintain the balance of power in Europe.

In 1737, however, the situation began to improve. Benjamin Franklin cheerfully added to his already incredible number of duties that of postmaster of Philadelphia. Typical of Franklin, he not only began at once to reorganize the system on a more efficient basis, but he soon found a way to make the job profitable not only to the Crown but to himself as well.

In his *Autobiography* he explained how he did it:

"I accepted it readily and found it to great advantage, for though the salary was small, it facilitated the correspondence that improved my newspaper, increased the number demanded, as well as the advertisements to be inserted, so it came to afford me considerable income."

At that time the postal laws made no reference to the carrying of newspapers, a fact that Franklin had been quick to see. In time, with Franklin to lead the way, other postmasters tried the same plan and began to print small papers of their own, which the poor postriders had to carry free. But they made up for this by becoming delivery boys for all sorts of supplies, a job for which they were paid. In fact, the duties of postriders were so vaguely defined that one of them was actually asked to bring along a couple of oxen on his next trip!

Benjamin Franklin was always on the lookout for new and better ways of doing things. He had not only a great deal of imagination, but he had practical common sense to channel it in useful ways and courage in putting it to work. So he set up the first night mail between Philadelphia and New

York. The colonists were wild with much the same kind of excitement that people felt recently over the first flight of man into space. They said that Franklin had practically abolished space and time. Why, they declared, you could send a letter to New York from Philadelphia and have an answer back within thirty-six hours! It was enough to make a man dizzy just to think about it.

Franklin is often regarded as the first American Postal Inspector. He took the haphazard methods he found and turned them into an efficient system. He set up a brand-new method of keeping accounts; he established new post offices, auditing their accounts much as Postal Inspectors do today to make sure that all money was accounted for.

By 1753 he was Deputy Postmaster General, a Crown appointment. He set out to visit every post office in the colonies and he saw them all, with the single exception of Charleston. With his prodigious energy he planned new and better routes and methods to speed the sending of the mails. Where in the past a man had ridden post between New York and Philadelphia once a week, he now made three trips.

Always Franklin's immense curiosity and his active intelligence were keenly alert. In 1764 the British Postmaster General called Franklin's attention to a situation that puzzled him. Why, he asked, did it take a fast mail packet longer to sail from Falmouth, England, to New York and Philadelphia and Boston than it took a slow merchant ship from London, though the latter had to come a much longer distance?

Franklin did not know, but the problem interested him. He said that he would find the answer—and he did. He always made a point of talking to all kinds of people because their different ways of life interested him. One day he was chatting with a Nantucket whaling captain and it occurred to him to put the problem to the man who knew the ways of the sea.

That was easy, the whaling captain replied promptly. They had "got in the stream." What stream? A current of warm water, the captain explained, that ran along the American coast. No one knew much about it.

So Franklin set to work to study this unknown warm stream and he was the first to chart it. Today it is better known as the Gulf Stream. This may be a far cry from carrying the mail, but it was all in the day's work to Franklin.

In 1773 Hugh Finlay took over Franklin's job. Poor Finlay had a hard time of it. Everything seemed to be against him. We know about his trials and tribulations because he kept a detailed diary of everything that happened. He was one of the first of many Postal Inspectors to leave an account of the adventures encountered in the course of their work. There can be few fields of government service, even including the military, in which public servants have had more varied and exciting experiences during their career.

But to return to Finlay. To begin with, the colonists were in a state of unrest. In another three years the American Revolution would break out in a blaze, and already there were many signs of disaffection. Finlay, however, was a Loyalist, devoted to the Crown and completely without sympathy for any talk of revolution or rebellion against the laws of the mother country.

He was a conscientious man and he was given an incredibly hard and difficult task to perform, that of blazing a post road from Quebec to "Bostontown," as it was then called. Leaving Quebec on September 13, Finlay set out with two other white men and eight Indian guides. They traveled in canoes during the day and at night one of the Indians made a map of the way they had come, drawing with charcoal on birch bark.

In spite of hardship, discomfort and danger, Finlay went doggedly on with his job of Postal Inspector. It wasn't going to be his fault if the mails didn't get through. Each day he set down a faithful account of the problems he had met and of his achievements. But there were all sorts of difficulties he had not foreseen. For instance, when he tried to survey the post roads in the South, he found they weren't really roads at all.

"Horses sank to the bellies in swamps," he wrote dismally, "and broke their legs in holes in corduroy roads." After long, exhausting days of that heartbreaking labor, there was not even any rest or comfort to look forward to in the evenings. All he could find was a "poor, sandy, barren, gloomy country with huts for taverns."

Poor Hugh Finlay! One time he reported: "The post rider Noble is not able to go through Marblehead because he would be obliged to undergo the ceremony of smoking [sic], that is, to be fumigated with brimstone because of the smallpox in Salem. As he is of a weakly constitution he cannot submit to it."

To add to all his other troubles, the outraged Loyalist reported in some bewilderment that the unruly colonists were trying every possible trick to avoid paying postage to the Crown.

"It is deem'd necessary," he wrote in great indignation, "to hinder all acts of Parliament from taking effect in America. They are, they say, to be governed by laws of their own framing and no other."

Two years later, in 1775, the Continental Congress took matters into its own hands and decided to establish its own postal system, independent of the Crown. Of course, Benjamin Franklin was elected to serve as the first American Postmaster General.

By 1793, when the colonists had become a nation in earnest, after the turmoil of the Revolution and a long period in which each colony was more concerned with its own interests than with the reality of Union, the United States Post Office was established through legislation passed by Congress. For the first time postal employees were required to take an oath of fidelity.

That was still a period, all over Europe and England, as well as in the New World, when punishment was drastic and terrible. For years to come in England people were transported or hung for minor theft. So the first penalty provided by law in America for the theft of valuable letters was death. This law stayed in effect for six years, when it was modified to public whipping. Much later it was again altered to imprisonment.

Anyone who has visited the reconstructed villages of Williamsburg in Virginia or Old Sturbridge in Massachusetts has seen the stocks, the pillory, and the whipping post, where public punishment was meted out. Today these structures are used by tourists as backgrounds for funny snapshots to send back home, but in their own day they were anything but funny to their victims.

Unhappily punishment, however drastic it is, does not appear to be a deterrent to crime, so, when Jonathan Burral became Assistant Postmaster General in 1789, he discovered that the service was completely inadequate. There were not enough postmasters, not enough roads, and many of the postmasters had been dipping their hands into the till of the United States Post Office, without being punished at all.

Nor was it the postmasters alone who were at fault. Robbery of the mails began to loom as a real problem. Highwaymen were appearing all over the colonies, robbing the unarmed postriders. As a result, in April 1793, Postmaster General Pickering appointed a man whose job it was to catch these "villains robbing the post." The man was Noah Webster, later to be known as the great compiler of the first American dictionary.

Even with vigilant men like Noah Webster trying to catch the "villains robbing the post," there was still too little protection for the mails and small reason for believing that letters would reach their destination safely. Things reached such a point—of course, there were no such things as money orders at the time—that when people wanted to send money by mail the best security they could achieve was to cut the bank notes in two pieces, mail one half, and, when that had arrived, send the other.

In fact, the miracle is that any mail reached its proper destination. All sorts of unexpected problems cropped up. For example, in 1797 the Post Office Department had to be moved temporarily from Philadelphia to Trenton because of an outbreak of yellow fever.

The South was still largely a wilderness. Once the mail through Kentucky was held up for months because the postriders could not find the distributing office at Moffats!

During the War of 1812 the Post Office Department assigned its inspectors to Port Tobacco and Point Lookout in Maryland where they were to watch the maneuvers of the British fleet in the Potomac through glasses and make daily reports.

On May 16, 1812, the Postmaster General wrote to Richard Bache, postmaster of Philadelphia:

"Sir:

"As you are of opinion that a lamp will 'add to the safety of your office and the convenience of the public,' you can purchase oil out of the funds of your office, and make the experiment, which can be discontinued if it does not prove to be useful."

A couple of years later a Vermont post office was made an exchange office for mail from Canada. The post office employees were ordered to soak all the deerskin mailbags in oil to protect the mails from water while the post horses were swimming across streams.

And in 1825 a request was made by the people of New York for a post office in the upper part of the city near Chatham Square. This request was turned down coldly by the postmaster. A town as small as New York, he declared, would not need such a post office, which would be more of a nuisance than an accommodation.

Early in the eighteenth century, as the bulk of the mail grew heavier along the eastern seaboard, the postriders began to be replaced by the mail coach.

These Conestoga wagons were big and awkward; they were springless, and the wheels had tires with hardwood on the rims. For over a hundred years, however, these slow, uncomfortable wagons jolted up and down the seaboard and then, as prairie schooners or covered wagons, they made the long dangerous journey across the continent to the Pacific Coast.

III ☆ The Ear Biters

A POSTAL INSPECTION service was established by the first American Congress, though it was not until 1829, under President Andrew Jackson, that the Postmaster General became a member of the Cabinet.

One of the functions of the Postmaster General was to provide trained men to inspect the service and its operations. Long before they were called Postal Inspectors, men whose duties were much the same were known as Secret Agents.

One of the first of these of whom we know was Ebenezer Grogan. In 1807 he was given the job of tracking down thieves who robbed the mails. It is interesting to see that the methods he used then were similar to those employed today, although, of course, the modern Postal Inspectors have more elaborate paraphernalia and greatly improved and faster methods of communication.

Once Ebenezer was told to go to Nashville, Tennessee, using a false name. There he was to meet the mail stage when it arrived and examine every package. He was instructed that if any mail had been opened he was to make a note of the post office from which it had been sent and then make sure the mail went on to its destination. From Nashville he was to take the mail stage on to Knoxville, where he was to repeat this performance. From there he was to accompany it from one post office to another until, he was told, "you discover where the villainy is committed."

For Ebenezer, as for the Postal Inspectors of today, the full responsibility of handling the job was left to him. The Secret Agent was, as his instructions said, to "depend on your own judgment and discretion and the authority with which you are clothed." He was also told that he could promise the driver of the mail stage "the compliment of a dollar." Ebenezer himself was to receive three dollars a day plus his expenses. And he was warned, as all modern Postal Inspectors are warned: "Be careful not to read, nor permit any other person to read, any of the letters the sack of which has been violated."

Ebenezer appears to have been a good man. By 1819 the Postmaster General, R. J. Meigs, was able to say: "Since I have been head of this Department not one instance of a violent robbery of the mail has occurred where the perpetrators have escaped apprehension, conviction and punishment."

Not that Ebenezer was the only agent to be doing fine work, of course. Three years later Meigs said of another agent, named Bailey: "Bailey has been the means of prosecuting to conviction more offenders against the Post Office Law, within the past ten years, than all other persons in the United States unconnected with the Department."

But even with this stirring record, it was not until 1840 that the office of Special Agent was created, the first group of technically trained investigators whose job was to protect the United States mails.

In 1840 Postmaster General Amos Kendall set up a new position in the Post Office Department which he called a "Special Agent." His purpose was laudable; he wanted to provide an inspection service that would really protect the mails against a growing band of highwaymen, mail robbers, and dishonest postmasters.

Unfortunately the department was troubled and handicapped by political appointments, and the Special Agents began to fall into disrepute because they became involved in politics. In fact, sometimes their interference at the polls led to violence. The climax came when a Special Agent stuck a knife into the ribs of a member of the opposition party and another overenthusiastic Special Agent attacked his enemy by biting off his ear.

The public was aroused by this incident, protested vigorously, and for a long time afterward referred to the Special Agents as "the Ear Biters."

Five years later all of them were discharged and men of high personal qualifications were selected. One of the most famous of these was J. Holbrook, who later wrote an account of his experiences called *Ten Years Among the Mail Bags*. As a matter of fact, a number of men have written accounts of their work in the Postal Department which provide valuable information about their methods, the variety of their activities, and the times in which they lived. Some of them we will meet later in this story.

Holbrook proved to be a fine agent and an expert thief catcher, but, unfortunately, when he wrote about his experiences he did it in such a flowery style that much of his book seems, unintentionally, very funny today. But what counted was the job he did.

One of the first problems that Holbrook encountered was a complaint that mail was being stolen from a certain vicinity where there was a school. Money sent to the pupils was disappearing and there were no funds for their tuition.

"The thefts," Holbrook wrote, "were up to me to solve."

All that he knew for certain was that the thefts were occurring somewhere along the route "extending from Boston to a well-known and flourishing island in one of the New England states." Holbrook was always careful not to identify too clearly either the place or the guilty individual because, at the time he wrote his memoirs, the families of the guilty ones were still living and he did not want to cause them embarrassment.

When he reached the town where the school was situated he met the postmaster, a man of seventy who had a fine reputation in the neighborhood. Holbrook went back and forth over the route, trying to discover where the thefts occurred. Of course, he traveled incognito, because he did not want to forewarn the thief of his activities and suspicions.

One of the Special Agent's greatest trials, he complained, was that often when he was investigating mail thefts and traveling under another name, some well-meaning but thoughtless acquaintance would call out jovially and at the top of his voice, "Well, Holbrook, caught any mail thieves lately?"

Once his identity was discovered, of course, his job became much more difficult to accomplish, because the thief had been warned and had an opportunity to cover his tracks or to vanish altogether.

"One of the missing packages contained several $20 notes on one of the Boston banks," Holbrook related.

At that time an exhibition was being held in the town. It had attracted a number of visitors, which complicated the task. Holbrook began the long, patient checking that accounts for the high record of convictions of the postal service, for nothing is left to chance and there are no loose ends which the investigators have failed to tie up.

From one store to another Holbrook plodded, asking at each one whether they had received any $20 notes like the one he was seeking. Several of these turned up, so he knew that the thief must have been in the town.

Who had paid out the notes? In each case the description was the same. It fitted to a tee the postmaster in the very town where the money had disappeared.

Remembering the man's fine reputation and his widespread popularity, the Special Agent knew that he had to make doubly sure before accusing him. He asked for a detailed description of the way the man was dressed. This time he was told of an unusual coat worn by the individual who had had the bank notes in his possession.

There was only one tailor in the town and Holbrook went to see him. The Special Agent described the coat. Had he made it?

"Yes," the tailor said at once. "I made that coat for the postmaster."

Holbrook then went to call on the young district attorney and laid the case before him. The attorney's name was H. Franklin Pierce and he was later to become President of the United States. There again he was to play a part—but a very unusual one—in the affairs of the United States Post Office, by signing the most ridiculous bill ever designed to expedite the American mails.

As Holbrook tells the story: "The following facts were now in my possession. M. F. was in the same town where the exhibition was held. His general appearance corresponded to that of the person who exchanged the notes. His position as postmaster gave him sufficient opportunities to have committed the robberies."

But the Special Agent could not bring a case to court on mere supposition. He had to have proof to substantiate his arguments. So Holbrook made up some dummy packages and a letter in which he placed $50 in marked money. Mr. Pierce, the young district attorney, was to travel on the mail stage that carried the letter on from the suspected post office while Holbrook would follow on horseback.

The mail stage stopped at the post office presided over by the suspected man and then went on. Immediately Holbrook joined Pierce on the stage and they went through the mailbag. The letter containing the marked money was not there. That settled it.

They returned to the post office and searched the postmaster, who made a great display of indignation. The money was found in his wallet. Another crooked postmaster had been caught.

A few years later Holbrook handled the case of the man who, as he put it, was "below suspicion." For some time large sums of money had been disappearing somewhere along the mail route by train from New York to Boston, often thousands of dollars in a single night. Eventually the searchers were able to eliminate the train crew, then the employees of the Boston post office. Finally the search was narrowed down to New York where the financial position of all night clerks was scrupulously checked to discover whether any of them had acquired any sudden wealth for which they could not account. But the night clerks, too, were all proved to be innocent.

Meanwhile the thefts continued. At last Holbrook turned his attention to the one man whom he had not even considered because his position was such a minor one that he seemed to be below suspicion. This was a night porter named Pat in the New York Post Office.

One morning, when Pat went off duty, Holbrook was waiting. He trailed the night porter to a store. After Pat had left, Holbrook went in. There he found a bill with an identifying mark. It occurred to him that the humble night porter had managed to steal well over $8,000. But what had he done with the money and how could the thefts be proved? Pat had no bank account and he did not appear to have an unusual amount of spending money.

This, by the way, has always been a helpful indication in catching thieves. They cannot seem to resist splurging with their stolen money, making lavish and conspicuous expenditures. This childish show-off quality frequently ends by causing their exposure and downfall.

Holbrook was sure of his man, but he did not have sufficient evidence for a court case and a conviction. He called on the police and asked for help. A policeman was assigned to work with him and for days they followed the unsuspecting Pat. He had a way of wandering off into the woods in Brooklyn and they thought he might have buried the money there. So they disguised themselves as hunters, to account for their presence, and followed him into the woods. But search where they would, they could not find any trace of the missing money, much of which was easily identifiable by number.

At last Holbrook and the policeman met Pat at the post office when he came on duty one night. They told him they knew he had been robbing the mails.

Pat denied it hotly. He was innocent, he declared.

They searched him. In his wallet they found $40 of the stolen money. Then they went carefully through his clothes. In the lining of his hat they turned up $165 more. At Pat's house, which they inspected thoroughly, they found $4,473. They had regained a fair part of the missing money and they had uncovered and ended the activities of the mail thief. But, considerably to Holbrook's chagrin, Pat slipped out of their clutches and escaped.

Holbrook was an unusual man in that he related truthfully and without excuses his failures as well as his successes. He told about another mail thief who escaped the law, although this time the Special Agent had succeeded in having his man arrested and locked up in jail. Next morning the thief had disappeared.

"How did this happen?" Holbrook demanded.

"Well," the jailor confessed in embarrassment, "last night the prisoner's wife came to visit her husband, carrying a big basket. When I looked in the cell this morning, there was the prisoner's wife lying on his cot. Her husband, dressed in her clothes, had walked safely out. Right in front of my nose."

But in spite of mishaps of this kind, Holbrook's record remained an extraordinary one, and the methods he conceived for detecting mail thieves have often since been put to use successfully. One of these was the preparation of a dummy package. A thief was usually smart enough to destroy the wrapping paper so there would be no evidence against him. But who would think of paying any attention to the string with which the package was tied? Holbrook measured the string carefully and tied knots at certain places so that he could identify it without difficulty. Many a mail thief was caught because he did not bother about a little piece of string.

Another idea occurred to Holbrook. Bank notes were often marked and they were comparatively easy to identify. Thieves were aware of this danger and, whenever possible, they managed to change the incriminating notes for unmarked money. But Holbrook went a step farther. He also marked coins. Once he caught a mail thief who had disposed of the marked bills but carelessly dropped a marked quarter in his pocket. Trapped by a quarter!

A final and amusing story concerns a young man who was seen night after night at a performance of *Uncle Tom's Cabin*. In the years before the Civil War, Harriet Beecher Stowe's sentimental story of slavery was immensely popular, both as a novel and as a play. In the latter the scenes of Eliza crossing the ice, pursued by bloodhounds, and particularly the one of Little Eva ascending into heaven, drawn by pulleys wielded by stagehands up above the stage, wrung tears from the audience and were sure to attract crowded houses.

What drew Holbrook's attention to the young man was not merely his constant attendance at the performance but the fact that he hired a box every night, a tremendous extravagance for a young man of no known income. On top of that, one evening he made a dashing gesture to attract attention to himself by tossing a gold bracelet on the stage at the feet of Little Eva, with whom he had fallen in love.

Holbrook was not interested in the love affair. What did concern him was where the young man was getting the money for the nightly box by which the *Uncle Tom's Cabin* company was profiting. He made it a point to investigate. Little Eva's admirer was robbing the mails in order to hire his box and provide the gold bracelet by which he meant to soften the heart of the actress.

Of course, many of Holbrook's cases lacked drama, though they paid off in the end by uncovering and stopping the robbery of the mails. There were long nights of watching, sometimes in dark rooms where he dared not move or make a sound, when his muscles grew cramped from being motionless, when the whine of a mosquito and its sting made it difficult to remain silent, when he had an almost irresistible inclination to sneeze or to cough.

There were patient hours and days and weeks of checking and rechecking his evidence, of waiting for a suspect to make a move that would betray him. There were the countless routine calls on stores and banks and friends or associates of the suspect, often with no result at all.

But, like the Postal Inspectors of today, Holbrook loved his job and he believed in it with all his heart. It was he who summed up one of the basic functions of the democratic system when he wrote:

"The laws of the land are intended to preserve not only the personal and material property of every citizen sacred from intrusion, but to secure the privacy of his thoughts, as far as he sees fit to withhold them from others."

IV ☆ The Man Who Never Gave Up

WHILE HOLBROOK was busy protecting the mails along the eastern seaboard, trouble was occurring in Ohio, where many packages seemed to be vanishing from the mail pouches by a kind of magic.

The mail was carried by the Ohio Stage Company, whose general agent was General Otto Hinton. Hinton had spent most of his life in handling the United States mails. When he was just a boy he started as a mail rider. He had delivered the very first mail pouch to reach Columbus, Ohio, when it was a solitary log hut set down in the midst of a forest. From this lowly beginning he had advanced steadily, finally reaching the position of general agent of the company.

As the mail thefts became more frequent and more serious in extent, a Special Agent named Thomas P. Shallcross was called in to investigate. When he found out what the situation was he became as puzzled as everyone else. It really seemed that the robberies could not occur, and yet they did.

This was the position. All mail pouches were locked at

the post office and then stowed in the front boot of the mail coach, under the very feet of the driver. When the pouches reached their destination they were still locked, they had not been cut open, but the money had been removed. Therefore it seemed as though the thefts simply couldn't happen.

Naturally Shallcross met Hinton and discussed the robberies with him. To the surprise of the Special Agent, Hinton did not seem to want to talk about the matter at all. In fact, he left Shallcross as soon as he could. This was curious behavior in a man who should be particularly anxious to have the thefts solved and his company cleared of all blame. Of course, it was not Hinton who had asked to have the robberies investigated.

Shallcross's suspicions were aroused, but when he mentioned them he was assured that Hinton was above suspicion. In any case, he was warned, it was not wise to accuse a man in his high position of a crime. Shallcross made clear that he was neither impressed nor frightened by any man's position or influence. His job was to protect the mails no matter who was involved.

Well, then, he was asked, if Hinton was guilty, as the Special Agent seemed to believe, how had he managed to commit the thefts?

"The mail pouches are intact when they arrive," Shallcross said. "They have not been cut open. Therefore they must have been unlocked."

"But," he was told, "Hinton does not have access to keys that unlock the mail pouches."

Shallcross was not easily defeated. He believed that Hinton had taken advantage of his position to rob the mails, but there appeared to be no way of proving it. Keys? Suddenly he remembered that a set of keys to mail pouches had been stolen the year before. It stood to reason that they must be in the possession of the mail thief.

But still, even if Hinton had acquired the set of keys, how was the thing being worked? The fact remained that the driver of the stage rode from one post office to the next with his feet practically resting on the mail pouches.

Then, on an August night of 1850, it happened again. The mail pouches were robbed somewhere on the road between Zanesville, Ohio, and Wheeling, West Virginia. They had been intact when they left Zanesville and were put on the coach. They had been rifled when they reached Wheeling.

Shallcross heard of the theft and set out to follow the route of the stage. Somewhere along the line the theft had occurred. At an inn at Morristown, Ohio, which was also used as a stage stand, the Special Agent made inquiries.

"Has General Hinton been here recently?"

"Why, yes, he was here on August twenty-third."

Shallcross pricked up his ears. The mail robbery had occurred on August 22.

Could he see the room in which Hinton had stayed?

Of course.

The room had long since been cleaned up, but one thing had been overlooked—the fireplace. Carefully raking over the ashes, Shallcross found "scorched pieces of letters, post bills, strings and lumps of sealing wax," which had failed to burn. He was now sure of the guilt of his man, but he still did not know how Hinton had obtained access to the locked mail pouches.

Then Shallcross questioned the driver of the mail stage.

Yes, the driver said promptly, General Hinton had traveled on the stage with him. Why not? After all, he was general agent of the company. But that particular night he happened to be tired so he decided that he would crawl in under the canvas top at the back of the stage and try to get some sleep. He had asked whether he could use one of the mail pouches as a pillow.

The picture was now clear and the mysterious robberies of the mail were explained. Concealed from the driver by the canvas top of the stage, it had been easy for General Hinton to unlock the mail pouch with one of the keys he had stolen a year before and remove, at his leisure, anything that looked promising, leaving the pouch locked and presumably untouched behind him.

It happened that one of the stolen items was a large bundle of bank notes. By this time Hinton had gone on to Cleveland. Shallcross wrote to the Cleveland postmaster, described the money that had been stolen, and asked that Hinton be shadowed. The postmaster called a United States marshal and together they kept an eye on the suspected man. Hinton's first action was to drop in to see a broker with whom he deposited the stolen money. The two men followed him, examined the money, and arrested him.

Shallcross was delighted; but, as it happened, his troubles had just begun. Hinton escaped. He was recaptured and re-arrested. He put up a bond and then escaped again. Shallcross still followed grimly.

Then Hinton, desperate to get rid of this human bloodhound, pretended to commit suicide. The Special Agent didn't believe a word of it and continued to follow the traces of the fugitive. Shallcross was a man who never gave up, a tradition that Postal Inspectors follow to this day.

Nearly a year and a half later Shallcross, in disguise, had trailed Hinton to Havana, Cuba. Again the mail thief escaped. Next he turned up in Oregon. Like the Avenging Furies in Greek tragedy, Shallcross pursued him. Once more Hinton escaped, this time going to the Sandwich Islands.

Long afterward, penniless, a hunted man to the very end, he died in Australia.

Some years later, after the Civil War had been fought and during the presidency of Ulysses S. Grant, a strange case came to the attention of the government. A complaint was received from the West about Indian goods that had failed to arrive. The name of the Secretary of the Interior was signed to the contract for the Indian goods.

The Secretary was indignant. He had never seen the contract and he knew nothing about it. The Chicago firm handling the contract was enraged. Of course the Secretary of the Interior had signed the contract. In fact, President Grant himself had accepted a bribe of $5,000 to give them the contract.

At this news the angry President and the Secretary of the Interior went into action to clear up the whole ugly scandal. To begin with, they set the secret service to work. There were no results. Then they tried the first and most famous detective of his day, Alan Pinkerton. Still no results. Finally, aware of the brilliant work being done by the Special Agents of the United States Post Office, the furious government leaders turned to Thomas P. Shallcross.

The Special Agent at once went to Chicago to see the firm that had made the preposterous claim of having bribed the

President and received the signature of the Secretary of the Interior on a fraudulent contract.

The heads of the Chicago firm were likewise furious. A handsome man who called himself Carleton Brooks had called on them. He had assured them that he could arrange to get them the government contract if they would put up $5,000 with which to bribe President Grant.

The gullible businessmen apparently had more faith in the plausible and good-looking confidence man than they had in the integrity of the President of the United States. They gave "Carleton Brooks" the $5,000 in an envelope addressed to President Grant. The confidence man obviously exchanged envelopes and pocketed the money.

What interested Shallcross particularly was the fact that the swindler had written the contract on stationery with the letterhead of the Department of the Interior. How had he managed to get hold of it?

In the Interior Department, Shallcross began to ask his questions and describe the man Carleton Brooks.

"That sounds like my friend Captain Worms," one of the clerks in the department exclaimed.

"How did he happen to use department stationery?"

Well, the clerk explained rather apologetically, his friend Captain Worms had no office of his own, so he occasionally wrote his letters at the clerk's desk at the Interior Department and received answers there.

"Where is Captain Worms now?"

The clerk was uncertain. Not in town, he was sure of that. Had he any family? Oh, yes, a sister. In fact, a letter from his sister, addressed to Captain Worms in care of the clerk, had come to the Department of the Interior some time ago.

Did he remember the postmark? Fortunately the clerk did.

Shallcross promptly set out for the town where the sister lived. Captain Worms was not there, but Shallcross waited patiently. Sooner or later the swindler was bound to get in touch with his sister. At length a letter arrived for her with the postmark of a French lumber camp in northern Canada. Now, of course, Shallcross could not open the letter, even to obtain evidence, but at least he had the postmark as an indication of his man's whereabouts.

Off Shallcross went again. In the French-Canadian lumber camp he found Captain Worms, *alias* Carleton Brooks, this time passing himself off as a doctor and practicing medicine. And so ended the career of another swindler.

V ☆ Camels and the Jackass Express

Up to 1850 there was no regular system of mail delivery between the Mississippi Valley and Arizona, New Mexico, Colorado, and Southern Utah. In the early days, under Mexican rule, California had only two ways of getting mail: one was by supply ships that arrived from time to time but without any regularity. The other was rather a primitive system established by the army, which took mail from one military post to another and permitted the general public to use its facilities.

The military posts did their best, trying to deliver the mail. But the problem seemed to be insurmountable.

First of all, there was a vast stretch of unsettled country, towering mountains and broad rivers, uncleared forest and great stretches of desert without shade or food or water. There were snowdrifts higher than a man's head and quicksands to trap his feet. There were also great packs of wolves and herds of enormous buffaloes; there were grizzly bears that seemed almost impervious to bullets and that could crush a man in one terrible hug.

45

There were poisonous snakes, particularly rattlesnakes, so many of them that when the prairie schooners traveled across the plains, men had to walk ahead with long whips, beating them off so that the oxen or mule trains could pass in safety. For an animal bitten by a snake was often unfit to travel for some time, and the lives of the passengers depended on moving steadily onward toward their destination. There was no extra supply of food to waste in delay.

But more dangerous than unknown country and violent extremes of weather and wild animals were the men, savage and ruthless, who peopled the western plains and preyed on the mail coaches. It was hard to say which were the more to be feared: the Indians who murdered and scalped the white men or the reckless outlaws who were later to follow shipments of gold and mail coaches, ready to kill for the sake of lining their pockets.

The United States Post Office had very little money with which to cope with this vast problem. Moreover, few people in the East knew what conditions were in the country that stretched west beyond the Mississippi, and fewer had any practical idea of how to deal with them. A casual and irregular service was established between California and the Mormon settlement at Salt Lake City, popularly and rather scornfully known as "the Jackass Mail."

In 1851 the Postmaster General had to confess that the arrangements up to then were completely unsatisfactory. In his report he declared:

"The mail service in California and Oregon has been so irregular in its performance and so imperfectly reported that it is not included in this statement."

That was probably just as well. The postal system in the

West was in complete chaos. A Special Agent was sent out to learn just what the situation was. Considerably to his surprise, he found that post offices had been set up without any official authorization and manned by postmasters who had appparently appointed themselves! Financially these men were doing very well indeed, but no record of their illegal transactions had reached Washington.

Then Jefferson Davis, who was Secretary of War in the Cabinet of President Pierce, came up with a new idea. It sounded all right to the President, who signed a bill, in 1853, allowing an appropriation of $20,000 to purchase camels in Arabia. After all, camels had long been known as providing transportation that was satisfactory in the Sahara Desert, so why couldn't they be equally efficient in the "Great American Desert" of the Southwest?

So the comedy of the camels began. Seventy-five of them were bought and shipped from Arabia. They landed in Texas. The Sahara was made up of soft, shifting sands, but the Southwest was hard, rough, and stubbly ground. Shortly after they were put to work the camels were almost crippled by the unaccustomed terrain.

Those camels that could still walk after a short time had only begun their troubles. Horses and mules got one look at the strange creatures and took to their heels, causing dangerous runaways.

At length the whole plan for the "Lightning Dromedary Express," as it had been grandiloquently named, was abandoned as a dismal failure. Some of the camels were sold to circuses; some of them escaped from their baffled riders and wandered off. For years there were stories of lonely prospectors who claimed that they had actually seen a camel in the desert. Of course, not many sensible people believed such nonsense.

But still something had to be done about the mails. After the California gold rush in 1848 the people who had made the long transcontinental journey to the Pacific Coast began to demand some kind of mail delivery from the East. They were entirely cut off not only from family and friends but from all contact with the outside world.

Slowly a stage service, which carried mail as well as passengers, and sometimes gold, was set up. The starting point for the trip west was Independence, Missouri. The mail stages had to travel in convoys, each covered wagon heavily guarded. Obviously these slow, cumbersome vehicles, pulled by oxen or Missouri mules, had no possible chance of running away from attack by gunmen or Indians on horseback. All they could depend on was a watchful group of armed men who were quick in action and quick on the trigger. Usually there were eight to ten sharpshooters with each convoy, which, at most, made a distance of twenty miles a day.

These prairie caravans consisted as a rule of twenty-five covered wagons, each drawn by twelve oxen, with twenty to twenty-five extra oxen for use in case of accident.

It was a slow business traveling across the plains, but the real problems, the back-straining labor, came in braking the great wagons when the road pitched steeply down into the gulches or pushing and straining from the back to help the oxen when the wagons had to make a sharp climb upward.

Stages carrying mail started as early as 1849, and later there was an overland stage to Salt Lake, which made the trip once a month. By 1854 the government gave a mail contract that paid $80,000 a year to John Butterfield, who was to see that the mail went overland from St. Louis to San Francisco by way of El Paso.

A new and hazardous job for the Special Agent was that of helping to guard these jolting, crawling prairie schooners, eyes on the horizon in search of raiders. Sometimes they shot it out; sometimes they tracked down white thieves and red marauders; often they had to bury the dead. But always their chief job was to save the mail and see that it went through to its destination.

The first people to make that trek west did so in a spirit of high adventure. For those who followed, a few years later, that adventurous spirit hardened to a grim determination to stick it out and reach their goal. For by 1852, particularly along the Oregon Trail, the sides of the road bore mute testimony to the fate of those who had gone ahead. The whole trail seemed to be lined not only with graves but with skeletons that had bleached in the sun. Even more disheartening than this was the sight of the covered wagons that had turned back and passed them, headed for the East again. These were survivers of a cholera epidemic.

What kept the western caravans headed steadily toward their destination was the magnificent and courageous pioneer spirit that was eventually to build the West. Of colorful characters and western heroes there were to be a great number, but their contribution, on the whole, was merely to the drama of the West and to creating the basis for the "Westerns" of today; it was the sturdy pioneer, patient, brave, hardworking, with a vision of a new civilization and a better life built of laborious toil and independence, who really was responsible for the opening of the West.

The chief exception, perhaps the most deservedly popular

man of his day, was that quiet and unostentatious scout, Kit Carson, the first man ever to carry the mails from coast to coast. If his exploits were later publicized, it was not by Kit Carson himself. It was Frémont and Senator Benton who exploited the qualities of this remarkable scout of the plains, well aware that he epitomized the spirit of the West at its best. They made use of his reputation to dramatize to the American people the qualities of the new and unknown country in order to encourage its permanent settlement.

Kit Carson, born in 1809, was not, in appearance, the typical western hero. He was small, towheaded, bandy-legged, a quiet and laconical man. But when he spoke it was to the point.

Apprenticed to a saddler when he was a young boy, he ran away to the West. The indignant saddler put the following advertisement in a newspaper:

"Christopher Carson, a boy about sixteen years, small of his age . . . ran away . . . All persons are notified not to harbor, support, or subsist this boy under penalty of the law. One cent reward will be given to any person who will bring the said boy."

Fortunately that one-cent reward did not encourage any-one to report the young Kit who, in time, was to become the greatest scout of the plains. Although he could barely read or write, he learned to know the plains country, the animals, the Indians, as few people have ever known them. He could set his hand to anything, make a saddle or a gun or snowshoes or a canoe.

He might have come straight out of a James Fenimore Cooper novel. But he was also, in a sense, the first detective of the kind that Sherlock Holmes was described as being.

He could, according to Stanley Vestal, in his book *Kit Carson,* ". . . determine at a glance the species, age, sex, gait and sometimes the state of mind of whatever animal had made the tracks he found . . . He could recognize the hoofprints of his own horses . . . tell the tribe of the Indian whose mocassin track was under his observation."

He knew hardship and danger, hunger and pain. Once he was bleeding to death from a shot, and his life was saved only because the temperature was so bitterly cold that his blood froze!

It was on September 15, 1846, that Kit Carson left Los Angeles for Washington, D.C. He carried dispatches for the President, bearing the official announcement that California had become a territory of the United States.

That was two years before the California gold rush started, at a time when people traveled to California on sailing vessels by way of Cape Horn.

Kit made that transcontinental journey on horseback. When he reached Washington, months later, President Polk was so impressed by his incredible overland trip that he gave him a commission as Lieutenant of Rifles, promised him money for the trip, and started him back with his saddle-bags filled with mail.

The Senate refused to give him the commission and denied as well his right to be recompensed for any money he had had to use for expenses.

"I told Frémont I'd carry the mails through," Kit said laconically. "I reckon I'll do it. *Adiós.*" And the mails went through.

VI ☆ The Pony Express

IT WAS William H. Russell who suggested the idea of the Pony Express, a group of hardy young men on hardier ponies who would not only greatly outpace the stagecoaches but would be able to outpace Indians and gunmen alike and cut the time of mail delivery by many days. This was not actually to be a government institution. It was private enterprise, for which Russell obtained a government mail contract.

And so the most dangerous, dramatic, and colorful segment of American postal history came about. Gold had drawn people west, but it was the Pony Express that brought glamour. Long before the fast-shooting two-gun sheriff and the cowboy became symbols of the romance of the plains, the riders of the Pony Express established standards of horsemanship never to be equaled: hardier, more competent, more daring riders than any that followed them across the Great Plains.

Russell set to work to organize the Pony Express. From St. Joseph to Salt Lake City there were already stage stations, but these were twenty-five miles apart, which was too great a distance for a pony traveling at top speed. No rider was expected to go more than ten or twelve miles before he changed horses. The plan was that a rider would usually cover a maximum of seventy or eighty miles a day, changing mounts at least seven times.

Russell set up 190 relay stations between St. Joseph, Missouri, and Sacramento, California. He bought 420 wild mustangs, only half broken for riding, but fast and sturdy enough to stand the strenuous job. He hired 400 station keepers, whose chief job was to look after and feed the horses, particularly to protect them from thieves. Most important of all, he selected eighty riders. The latter were to be paid from fifty to one hundred and fifty dollars a month, depending on how long the trip was and how dangerous it might prove to be. This was excellent pay at a time when twenty dollars a month was considered adequate for a stage driver over equally dangerous terrain.

The 1,900 miles from Sacramento to St. Joseph was covered by the Pony Express in nine days and twenty-three hours, and it cut the time of mail delivery from San Francisco to New York by ten days.

Because of the high pay for the riders, the cost of sending a letter by Pony Express was five dollars a half ounce, which was later reduced to one dollar. The paper was the lightest obtainable; the mail pouches were very small, covered with oilskin, and locked into a compartment in the saddlebag.

The Pony Express riders were a colorful lot, magnificent horsemen, tireless, fearless, quick-witted and self-reliant. Originally they were supposed to be over twenty years of age and to weigh no more than one hundred and twenty-five pounds, though exceptions had to be made to both rules occasionally. How many of their names have come down to us in almost legendary form: Joaquin Miller, "Pony Bob" Haslan, Buffalo Bill Cody, Wild Bill Hickok.

In his book *Roughing It,* Mark Twain described the thrill of seeing the Pony Express in action:

"Here he comes! Every neck is stretched farther, and every eye strained wider. Away across the endless dead level of the prairie a black speck appears against the sky and it is plain that it moves. Well, I should say so. In a second or two it becomes a horse and rider, rising and falling, rising and falling—sweeping toward us, nearer and nearer—growing more and more distinct, more and more sharply defined—nearer and still nearer, and the flutter of the hoofs comes faintly to the ear—another instant, a whoop and a hurrah from our upper deck, a wave of the rider's hand, but no reply, a man and a horse burst past our excited faces, and go winging away like the belated fragment of a star!"

The first day of the Pony Express Service was set for April 3, 1860, when, at the same time, a rider was to start east from Sacramento and another to start west from St. Joseph, Missouri. Everyone in St. Joseph seemed to be waiting for the big moment when the train from the East would arrive with the mail. A laughing, cheering mob gathered around the young rider who stood impatiently, his pony already saddled.

Then, as now, Americans were enthusiastic souvenir hunters, and finally the harassed pony had to be rescued and put back in the stable. People had pulled out so many hairs from its mane and tail as mementos that there were enough of them to make souvenir rings and watch chains for a long time to come. The enterprising pluckers sold their souvenirs for a high price.

From the beginning, as Joaquin Miller pointed out, there was a "die-in-the-saddle" spirit among the riders. Actually Joaquin—a name he gave himself after he became a poet—was not with the Russell outfit. He was employed by Isaac V. Mosson, of Walla Walla, Washington, who owned a thriving but independent pony express of his own, which carried mail from the mining regions of Montana and Idaho to Walla Walla. According to Mosson, Joaquin "had one little pony and five dollars in cash, but he could ride well and was a hustler. I gave him an interest in the business."

Joaquin was probably the only one of the Pony Express riders who wrote poetry in his off time. In fact, he once read a book of poems by a young woman and, being a man of action as well as a poet, he set off promptly to see her and married her in three days, after threatening away her admirer with his revolver.

But even for Joaquin the poet the job was incredibly rugged. The winter of 1861-62, he related afterward, was the coldest ever known in that section. On one occasion, when the snow was piled high: "I had walked all the way from Florence to Walla Walla on this crust, nearly 200 miles as the train ran, with nearly 100 pounds of gold dust and letters on my back."

The "die-in-the-saddle" quality mentioned by Joaquin Miller was literally demonstrated by a young Mexican rider for the Pony Express who rode into Dry Creek station, clinging to his saddle horn. He had been caught by an insurgent Indian tribe, the Paiutes, and wounded so severely that he died soon after he reached Dry Creek. But he had hung on until he reached his destination and he had brought the mail through with him.

In fact, in spite of the dangers encountered almost daily, only one mailbag was ever lost by the riders of the Pony Express in the entire course of its existence!

Today, with superhighways extending from coast to coast, it is difficult to imagine the pathless wilderness through which these sturdy and competent young riders hurled their ponies at top speed. In winter there were the great mountain passes where a man must lead his horse through snow piled many feet high, often concealing dangerous crevasses, with bitter wind cutting at man and beast, and temperatures dropping far below zero. In the spring there were land and rock and snow slides. Farther south, in the desert, there was baking, relentless heat that soared far over a hundred degrees and no water except for what could be held in a light canvas bag, which the rider could carry on his saddle horn. Every ounce of weight counted.

It was a lonely life: the high scream of wind over the prairies, the howling of wolves, the wild carrying cry of coyotes. There were few human voices. A wild gallop of ten miles, a leap out of the saddle onto a fresh pony that was saddled and waiting, a hurried word, then on to the next relay station.

The relay stations themselves provided none of the creature comforts we take for granted today. The men lived in frail huts with a little handmade furniture. Their diet, according to Sir Richard Burton, famous translator of the *Arabian Nights*, "was sometimes reduced to 'wolf mutton' or a little boiled wheat or rye; the drink was brackish water."

Here they lived in freezing cold or scorching heat, without friends or help in case of need, with constant danger threatening their survival, and only a few scattered and distant army posts to attempt the protection of a vast territory where no means of communication existed.

Along with their major job, the care and feeding of horses, the station keepers were often busy protecting the stock from Indians, who would steal anything they could get their hands on, or patiently rebuilding the flimsy stations that were burned down by them.

On one of his trips for the Pony Express, "Pony Bob" Haslan found one relay station after another burned to the ground. The station keepers had been killed and scalped. Without being able to change horses or stop for food or rest, young Haslan had to ride 380 miles before he found a station still standing, and always with the grim evidence that the Indians were just ahead of him on their destructive raid.

On another occasion Pony Bob ran into an ambush of thirty Paiutes. All of them had rifles and they were ready to use them. The next relay station was more than three miles away and the Indians were between him and the station. There was no time to weigh his chances. Instead of trying to retreat, he pulled out his revolver and spurred his horse straight toward the Indians. Thirty to one!

"You pretty good fellow," the chief called. "You go ahead."

Pony Bob did not stop to discuss the matter. He went ahead.

There was one rider who was nearly sucked into quicksands when a flash flood mired him in a stream. Another spent twenty-four hours in the saddle, carrying mail 120 miles through two to four feet of snow in zero weather. A third was most afraid of herds of buffaloes. These huge beasts roamed by thousands along the plains over the route of the Pony Express, and the man who rode into a herd was apt to be trampled to death. A fourth rider admitted that he was most alarmed by the great packs of wolves.

But the worst problem of all was the constant danger of Indian attack. In fact, just about two months after the Pony Express Service started its regular trips, it had to be suspended for four weeks in Nevada and Utah. The Paiutes had staged an uprising of such dimensions that the trips were too risky for the men, courageous as they were.

The first news that the Paiutes were on the warpath came when a rider reached Carson City, his horse in a lather, the rider in a state of exhaustion. The Williams relay station had been burned down. Five men, stock tenders and substitute riders, had been killed and scalped.

Then the Paiutes descended without warning on another station. Henry Wilson and Albert Armstrong, the station keeper and the stockman, were startled one morning when arrows began to pierce the thin walls of their cabin. They had just settled down to eat breakfast. The two men threw themselves on the floor, poured all the ammunition they could into their hats, and began to shoot through the cracks in the walls.

Wilson and Armstrong shot and reloaded as fast as they could, their eyes fixed in dismay on the diminishing supply of ammunition, ducking instinctively as arrows whanged into the boards over their heads or quivered against a wall.

When they had fired their last shots there was a moment's silence. Then the Paiutes, aware that they had run out of ammunition, broke into the flimsy little station. They bound their captives, tied them to a stake, and piled sagebrush around it. The two men knew that they were to be scalped and burned. At that moment the Indians caught sight of the food their captives had prepared for their breakfast but had had no time to eat. They sat down to enjoy it. The sight of their helpless victims and their awareness of what was going to happen to them seemed to add zest to their appetite.

Then—like one of those early movies where the cavalry dashes up at the last minute and another redskin bites the dust—the station was surrounded. Twenty soldiers from a nearby military post had ridden to the rescue. The Indians were captured and their prisoners were released.

By the way, it was not exclusively Indians who indulged in scalping. White men, too, frequently scalped their captives. As a matter of fact, there are still states in the Union that have on their statute books laws offering a bounty for scalps!

VII ☆ Wild Bill and Buffalo Bill

ONE OF THE stock tenders at the Rock Creek relay station on the Oregon Trail was James Butler Hickok, better known to us as "Wild Bill" Hickok.

Wild Bill was the most celebrated gunman of his day, so fast a shot that when he fired his two guns it sounded like a single shot. There were people who claimed that he had killed hundreds of men; he himself numbered his victims at "about a hundred, but always in self-defense." Such facts as can be obtained to substantiate these extravagant claims indicate that he probably shot no more than seventeen men.

There was no recognized law in the West except what men made for themselves. As a sheriff and, later, a marshal, Wild Bill managed to keep order among the lawless, chiefly because his reputation as a dead shot was known to everyone. When he moved along the streets of one of those western towns, his presence made it safe for the inhabitants. It was savage law, but at that time it was all they had.

Wild Bill comes into this story because he not only drove a mail stage but he became a substitute rider for the Pony Express, although he was much bigger and heavier than the pony riders were supposed to be.

By the time he was twenty-one he had already led a crowded life. As a fervent Abolitionist, he had helped many slaves to escape, driving them to safety at top speed while the slaveowners pursued him, firing at the helpless, terrified runaways.

He drove a mail stage through dangerous country for twenty dollars a month and his board. Always half gunman, half actor, he whipped up his horses before they reached Santa Fe so that they would arrive spectacularly at a hard gallop. Anyhow, he declared, it would "jolt the cricks out of the passengers' backs."

He acted as a sharpshooter to protect convoys of covered wagons. One time he was on horseback when a large grizzly attacked him. His horse reared, throwing him off. He emptied his pistol, but the grizzly kept coming. Then he pulled out his bowie knife. It was well known that any man would rather face two armed Indians than one grizzly—in fact, the Indians themselves thought the odds should be six men to one grizzly—but Hickok was alone, only a knife in his hand. When, later on, he was found, his scalp, arms, legs, and torso had been ripped by the bear, which lay dead beside his unconscious body.

His personal courage was magnificent. Once he had to undergo a serious operation. There were, of course, no anesthetics. When a spectator was overcome by the sight, Wild Bill impatiently asked for the lantern and held it steadily for the doctor who performed the operation.

He was an Indian fighter. He was later to be a spy on the Federal side in the Civil War, a scout for General Custer, and a marshal in Abilene, Kansas.

It was this particular phase of his life, the dead shot who

upholds law and order in a frontier community, that set the pattern for the countless "Westerns" which have been attracting people ever since. Night after night young and old sit glued to a television screen watching pale and often ridiculous imitations of the deeds performed by men like Wild Bill Hickok, though it is unlikely that anyone who was familiar with the frontier as it really was would ever recognize the originals.

Wild Bill was aware of his spectacular reputation and he acted the part. He was, according to everyone who saw him, a remarkable-looking man, with good features, the walk of a tiger, a perfect physique, and red-blond hair, which he wore hanging to his shoulders. That was typical of many of the hard-fighting, hard-shooting men, particularly the scouts, of the West. The long hair was a defiance of the Indians who liked to add scalps to their belts.

"Try to get this one," was the implied challenge of that flowing hair.

Professional writers who had gone West looking for dramatic material, old friends who knew him, the wife of General Custer, and a dozen others have drawn colorful and admiring pictures of Wild Bill and the flamboyant costume he affected.

The St. Louis *Republican* described Wild Bill:

"In physique he is as perfect a specimen of mankind as ever walked in mocassins or wore a pair of cavalry boots . . . and Bill is a dandy at all times—a regular frontier dude . . . quick to feel the cards or pull the trigger of a revolver. His hair is amber in hue, of the sort brightened but not reddened by the sunlight . . . His luxuriant growth of hair falls in ringlets over his shoulders . . . He walks like a tiger."

It is difficult to know today how much of Hickok was showman, how much genuine. It is a curious thing that the two most colorful men of the West, Wild Bill Hickok and William F. Cody, better known to us as "Buffalo Bill," equally divided their time between living the life of frontier scouts and then acting the same part in the theaters of the East.

Wild Bill was as aware as anyone of his fame and his dramatic appearance. It occurred to him that it would be a wonderful idea to show the people of the East what frontier life was like. So he collected a group of Indians and some wild buffaloes and with considerable difficulty brought them East. People would go far and pay a lot to see such novelties.

Once the buffaloes escaped and raced down the streets of a town in upper New York, pursued by yelling Indians. It provided a fine spectacle but, unfortunately for Wild Bill, the public was able to see it for nothing.

Hickok's next venture was in the Bowery Theater in New York, where he was asked to play himself in what must have been one of the worst melodramas ever written. At one point he was to clasp the distraught heroine in his arms and exclaim:

"Fear not, fair maiden! By heavens, you are safe at last with Wild Bill, who is ever ready to risk his life and die, if need be, in defense of weak and defenseless womankind."

This was too much for Wild Bill. When he reached that ringing speech, he was so embarrassed by the nonsense that he insisted on playing it in the dark.

By far the most famous of all the Pony Express riders was William F. Cody, better known as "Buffalo Bill." How many of the incredible stories told about him are true no one knows.

For over forty years he was to be a showman, traveling up and down the country with his Wild West Show. He always appeared in a big Stetson hat, a white buckskin suit with fringe on the sleeves, hair long and flowing, a mustache and goatee. The show featured the old Deadwood stagecoach pursued by howling Indians and ended in a tremendous uproar punctuated by blank cartridges.

How much of a showman Buffalo Bill was, even in his early years, it is hard to tell. He seems always to have been acting the part of Buffalo Bill. His *Autobiography,* of which he published a number of different versions over the years, only adds to the confusion. It credits him with fantastic exploits. According to one of these tales, he joined the Pony Express when he was only fourteen years old, made one run of 320 miles without a stop, was set upon by fifteen armed Sioux and outrode them.

There's one certainty about the boys of the Pony Express. They were such magnificent riders and so brave that that story could just possibly be true. But when we stop to remember that from 400 to 1,700 dime novels were written about Buffalo Bill during the course of his lifetime—the discrepancy in figures is typical of all stories about him—it is hard to separate fact from fiction. Perhaps he couldn't have done it himself.

Buffalo Bill was born in Iowa in 1846. Long before Russell established his Pony Express, he was running a freight service, using Conestoga wagons. Buffalo Bill claimed that he started working for Russell when he was only eleven years old. At fourteen he made that great ride of his, 320 miles, in twenty hours and forty minutes.

The popular name, "Buffalo Bill," was the result of young

Bill's hazardous job in killing buffaloes to supply fresh meat for the men working on the Kansas-Pacific Railway.

That was the day of Barnum, who proved that he could exploit practically anything; but, before he was through, Buffalo Bill had achieved almost as much fame and money by his own showmanship. Like Hickok, he invaded the New York theater where, also like Hickok, he played himself in a series of melodramas. Buffalo Bill had no illusions about his skill as an actor, but he was keenly aware of the fascination that western life had for people in the East. He was also, but unlike Hickok, an astute businessman. Slowly he began to create the kind of show he had long dreamed of, an out-of-doors show that would really dramatize details of Indian warfare. In the first place he called it "Scouts of the Prairie." Then he began to develop the "Buffalo Bill Wild West Show," which toured the country and Europe until early in this century.

Meantime, as dime novels dealing with his career began to pour from the presses, Buffalo Bill decided that he might as well write some of them himself. They were exciting but hardly to be relied on as a true description of the life he had known. He was aware of this himself and once wrote to his publisher:

"I am sorry to have to lie so outrageously in this yarn. My hero has killed more Indians in one war trail than I have killed in all my life."

Having conquered America, Buffalo Bill decided on a bold stroke. He would take his show to England and then to the Continent. After all, he had already met a number of Englishmen and Europeans who had made the long journey to see the West for themselves. He had set the pattern for the modern "dude" ranches when he entertained them.

His success abroad was far greater than even the most optimistic manager could have imagined. Queen Victoria saw the Wild West Show twice. Rosa Bonheur, the famous French artist, painted him on his horse.

In England he set a new pattern. The finale of the show was the pursuit of the Deadwood stagecoach, which he had bought, by Indians. In England, Buffalo Bill asked members of royalty if they would like to ride in the stagecoach for this grand finale. Like it? They loved it! From then on, wherever he went in Europe, there were members of royalty riding in the stagecoach as it thundered around the dusty track, accompanied by the howls of Indians and the crackle of blank cartridges. A grand time was had by all.

By the beginning of this century he was well into his stride. In a single year he cleared a profit of a million dollars. He had added to his cast now a group of men whom he called Rough Riders, a term that Theodore Roosevelt was later to use, Annie Oakley, known as "Little Missie," the girl dead shot, and her husband, Frank Butler. By a brilliant stroke he had also added Chief Sitting Bull, whom he agreed to pay fifty dollars a week and all expenses.

Chief Sitting Bull was no fool either when it came to money. He was willing to go along, playing himself, the villain in Custer's last stand at the Little Bighorn, but he insisted on an additional clause in the contract. He was to have the exclusive right to sell pictures of himself. Even staid Boston was delighted with Chief Sitting Bull. Indeed, someone remarked enthusiastically that he looked like Daniel Webster!

It is typical of Buffalo Bill that when he died his funeral

procession was rounded out by a parade of all the members of the Sells-Floto circus.

And then, when the transcontinental telegraph was completed, the Pony Express came to an end. Modern science had provided a means of communication so fast that not even the hardiest pony or the most determined rider could equal it.

VIII ☆ The Special Agents

FROM THE first day of its existence new problems have steadily arisen for the Postal Department, requiring new solutions. Somehow new solutions have been found to meet each situation.

One of the most exciting of these problems came up when gold was discovered at Deadwood in the Dakota Territory. Prospectors were busily engaged in getting it out. Outlaws were equally busy trying to hijack the gold shipments as they were sent out of Deadwood by stage. In fact, there were so many outlaws ready to rob stagecoaches that sometimes they shot it out among themselves for the privilege.

Because the stages also carried mail, the Post Office Department's Special Agents began to assume the job of escorting the stages at the head of a posse. When the outlaws escaped, the Special Agents kept on their trail and usually recovered the mail. In fact, they soon became known as such dead shots that outlaws learned to let the mail stages strictly alone, however tempting the fortune in gold that they might be carrying.

A case with a typical western flavor concerns a Special Agent, Inspector Charles Adams, who was sent to Deadwood to stop the thefts of registered mail from the stagecoaches.

Adams had come to the United States as a German immigrant and eventually he had been made adjutant general of the Colorado Territory. At the time he was sent to Deadwood he already had a history of great exploits behind him. He had, singlehanded, captured a Mexican gunman who had robbed the mails. He had headed a posse of soldiers in pursuit of some Paiutes who had not only robbed a mail coach but carried off a white woman. Now he had come to a frontier town famous for its lawlessness and its two-gun men.

One night Adams traveled on the Deadwood stage, presumably just another passenger, but actually, of course, waiting for possible attack by mail thieves. The stage was held up and Adams went into action. In the darkness he captured one of the highwaymen and had him locked up. The bandit never had a chance to see his face. Then Adams had a long whispered conversation with the sheriff, who laughed. It was a wonderful idea, he agreed.

A terrible uproar started outside the jail. Then the cell in which the bandit had been locked up was thrown open and Adams was pushed inside.

"I won't answer for your life," the sheriff shouted, "if the mob takes this jail. They are not in the mood to let off a horse thief."

The sheriff locked the door and Adams dropped down on the cot, apparently shaking with terror.

This was proof to the bandit that he and Adams belonged to the same brotherhood of outlaws. He began to boast of his own exploits. Horse thief, eh? Just small stuff. He and his gang stole gold. That was more like it.

Adams was duly impressed. His fellow "prisoner" told

him not only the names of the other members of his band but even where their hide-out was.

When the bandit had fallen asleep, the sheriff quietly unlocked the door and Adams slipped out. He collected a posse and began a search, which included a series of gun battles and extended from Dakota to Nevada. By the time it was over, all but two of the gang had been found, and most of them were either killed or wounded. No other mail stage from Deadwood was ever attacked again.

After the Civil War, David B. Parker was appointed Chief Special Agent for the United States Post Office, a position he held from 1876 to 1883. The scope of the job he had to do was enormous and he filled it magnificently. In time he became one of the finest detectives in America and his reputation was known and respected abroad.

Parker was not a man who had much opportunity to work at a desk. He seemed to turn up everywhere and take an active hand wherever it was needed, from riding at the head of a sheriff's posse in the West in search of outlaws who had robbed the mails to analyzing and solving a crime that had occurred 3,500 miles away.

The end of a war always leaves behind it chaotic and disorganized conditions and a rise in crime. This is as true for the victors as it is for the defeated. One of Parker's jobs was to investigate mail conditions in the West. There seemed to be no reliable reports either on the working of the mails or the efficiency of the system.

At that time, as now, the number of protectors of the mails for the whole country was extremely small. Parker had only ninety agents to handle this colossal job of supervising the

United States mail service from coast to coast.

Inevitably the service had deteriorated as a result of the Civil War, because the primary job of the Special Agents during the war years had been to establish military post offices and plan mail routes to meet constantly changing conditions.

Parker, like other Special Agents, left a story of his experiences in the post office. When the Civil War was over, his first job was to inspect the post offices, find ways of extending mail service in the West, and check on all violations of postal laws. That turned out to be quite an assignment.

Parker's job took him from Virginia to the Oregon Territory. His work was not limited to the exciting business of pursuing armed bandits at the head of a sheriff's posse and shooting it out in running gun battles, though he did that, too. He began to investigate the conditions under which the United States mails were actually being handled.

Because of the unsettled state of much of the West and the comparatively small staff of employees whom the Post Office Department could afford to hire, the mail was often turned over to carriers who worked independently but under a government contract. In principle these contracts were let out to the lowest responsible bidders. They were called Star Routes, because such services were indicated by the Post Office Department by three asterisks.

These Star Routes covered a total annual transportation of 75,000 miles, most of it wild land inhabited chiefly by unfriendly Indians. It seemed impossible to make a thorough check of conditions over so enormous a territory without any established communications system.

The Special Agents assigned to the task were horrified by

what they discovered. Corrupt politicians and crooked mail contractors had worked together in a gigantic swindle. Clerks in the Post Office Department were accepting bribes to let members of the Star Route fraud ring know of bids that had come in. Members of the United States Senate and of the House of Representatives were involved in the graft. The ring owned the newspapers in Washington, so that news of the swindle was blanketed off from the people in the capital. In time the Star Route frauds reached such a point that the grafters were completely protected by men in both the House and the Senate.

When Garfield was elected President, he became aware of the situation. The Chairman of the Republican National Committee, Senator Dorsey, appeared to be involved, but though the man held a high and influential position in his own party, Garfield did not hesitate. He appointed Thomas James to the office of Postmaster General.

"I have sworn to uphold the Constitution and the laws," Garfield told his new appointee. "I shall do my full duty. My instructions to you are, 'Cut the ulcer out, no matter whom it hurts.' "

Forty Special Agents, directed by P. H. Woodward, began to investigate not only the Star Route contracts but conditions in other post offices as well. They unearthed the whole ugly series of frauds. One contractor was collecting $30,000 a year, but all he ever carried with him was an empty mailbag. "Steamship companies" had contracts for mail deliveries, though one of them didn't own a ship, not even a canoe. The contractor, however, was growing rich on his income from "delivering the mail." Actually, when the mailbags arrived, they were simply thrown on the dock where they stayed until some boat could be persuaded to take them on.

In all the years of its existence the period between the Civil War and 1900 was the least creditable to the Postal Service, though it was also a period when it had some of its most brilliant and efficient inspectors. As is always the case, graft was permitted to exist simply because the public didn't care enough to do anything about it. No Special Agent, however honorable and brilliant he might be, could fight singlehanded against the apathy and indifference of the citizens.

Nonetheless, Parker managed to make a splendid personal record. One of his most famous exploits was his solution of a series of mail thefts occurring in Germany. For some time the German postal authorities had been concerned by the theft of registered letters between Hamburg and Berlin. They tried to solve the mystery themselves and failed. Then they called on the police. Germany had no such group as our Special Agents and, though police methods in Germany were thorough and painstaking, they were ineffectual in this case. The robberies continued.

At last the postal authorities wrote to Parker, whose reputation as a detective had spread far and wide, particularly for his solution of mail thefts and frauds. Parker decided that it was unnecessary to make the trip to Germany. He asked the authorities to send him a list of all the employees who handled the mail between Hamburg and Berlin, the hours they worked, and the time at which the mail vanished.

They secured the information and sent it back to Parker, who studied it. Then he made his report. He gave the German authorities the name of the one mail clerk who, because of the place where he worked and his hours on duty, had the best opportunity to steal the mail. He also outlined a proven method for obtaining evidence that this was the real thief.

The German officials were disappointed. This time the great detective had slipped up. The man whom Parker had indicated was one of their oldest employees and one whom everybody trusted. Nevertheless they decided to try the scheme suggested by Parker. They wrote some letters, marked in such a way that they could easily be identified, registered them, and then—found them in the possession of the very man whose guilt the Special Agent had detected from 3,500 miles away.

When Theodore Roosevelt became President, he began to search out the grafters who were preying upon the Post Office Department and, consequently, upon the American public as a whole. He appointed J. T. Bristol to take charge of the investigation. It was not pleasant for men to turn up dishonesty in their own department, but Bristol was stopped neither by fear nor favor. When his work had been completed, there were seventy-four indictments against men who had supplied post offices with equipment that was far too expensive to be justified or that was not even needed at all.

And with the end of that period of graft and the opening of the twentieth century there began the new period, that of the American Postal Inspectors, the world's greatest government law-enforcement agency, with an unparalleled record of achievement and personal honor.

Part II ☆ THE PRESENT

IX ☆ The Postal Inspectors

WE CALL THEM "America's Silent Investigators." Credit for their work is often taken by other agencies, but, though they are amused by the publicity seekers, they prefer to remain unknown.

When the Treasury Department established its Special Intelligence Unit to check on tax dodgers, it was no accident that they selected Postal Inspector E. T. Irey to organize the now-famous T men on the model of the Postal Inspection Service.

A great part of the strength of the Postal Inspectors grows out of their carefully preserved anonymity. Nonetheless, without boasting or fanfare, they have built such a reputation that even the most hardened criminal hesitates to tamper with Uncle Sam's mails. With a record of from 97.5 per cent to 99.1 per cent for conviction, in cases brought to trial, the Postal Inspectors almost invariably get their man, secure a conviction, and make sure that punishment follows in short order. The punishment is swift and terrible. There is no opportunity for a clever lawyer or a softhearted jury to affect the penalty. According to law, the armed holdup of an employee in charge of the United States mails is a mandatory sentence of twenty-five years in the penitentiary. There is no escape from this sentence, which has done much to make bandits think twice before they tamper with the mails.

There is another reason for their brilliant record. Postal Inspectors, since the day of Thomas P. Shallcross, never give up. They recognize no statute of limitations in the case of fugitives. No such case is ever closed until the man they are seeking has been arrested or is known to have died. A criminal, however daring, however reckless or sure of success he may be, hesitates for a long time before he takes a chance of bringing down on his head the full battery of talents of the most flexible detective force we have, knowing that, so long as he lives, he will never be free of pursuit, that the Postal Inspectors will never cease to track him down until he is captured.

Because of their remarkable training and the variety of methods they have at their disposal for tracing criminals, the Postal Inspectors are often called upon by other government agencies who have come up against a blank wall.

Of course, one of the obvious reasons for their strength is the fact that Postal Inspectors have at their disposal the widest possible source of publicity through the posters that appear in every post office in the country. We have all seen them, with a picture, a description of the man, his criminal record, and the word in large type: WANTED. Countless criminals have been recognized because of these posters and their whereabouts have been reported to the Postal Inspectors.

Another inestimable resource is the existence of the 200,000 mail carriers who serve the country. These men know, often by sight, always by name, all the people in their particular territory who ever receive any mail. It is almost impossible for a man to remain long concealed after his name and his picture have become known to the mail carriers because, in our modern world, the use of the mails is practically unavoidable. So the mail carriers, surely among the most peaceful and nonbelligerent of our public servants, constitute a whole army of detectives in themselves.

The work of the Postal Inspectors falls into two major divisions. The first consists of an annual survey of every post office to go over the books, make sure that all money and stamps—some twenty eight billion stamps a year—are accounted for, to check on the efficient operation of the post office, the competency of the postmaster, and the prompt distribution of the mail, to correct inadequate mail handling and suggest methods of improving it.

The second division of their work consists of criminal investigations, which Postal Inspectors are required to carry through from the gathering of the evidence and the arrest of the suspect to preparing reports and presenting the case in court. These investigations cover a broad range, one that grows broader every day, as men ingeniously find new ways of rooking the public and the Postal Inspectors counter with new ways of stopping them.

Their investigations cover theft of the mails, fraud in countless forms, forgery of stolen money-order forms, the use of threats and blackmail or poison-pen letters, and many forms of violence by mail. All this work, for the whole United States, is done by one thousand Postal Inspectors who protect the world's biggest business. But each of these men seems to be an army in himself. Indeed, he has to be. Postal Inspectors, who may have a case load exceeding one hundred and fifty cases at one time, determine for themselves what cases they will handle, as well as when and how they will handle them. They assume full responsibility for their actions and the results. Small wonder then that they put in an average work week of fifty-three hours, though they receive no pay for overtime or extra money for night service.

Inspectors have written instructions on the techniques for investigating every type of crime, but they rely on their own intelligence, training, and observation and, of course, increasingly on their five scientific laboratories, where science proves to be the greatest detective of all.

Naturally men constantly overburdened with a heavy load of cases find that their work may take them anywhere at any time to look for evidence or to pursue criminals. One of the cardinal rules of the Postal Inspection Service, therefore, is that each man must keep his superior informed at all times as to where he may be reached, because his life is one of constant emergencies in which no time is to be lost.

Because the position of Postal Inspector demands exceptional qualities of integrity and self-reliance, as well as a flexible, observant mind that can be called on for high detective ability often under novel or unforeseen conditions, the men appointed meet the highest standards of any government agency. Since the Post Office Department has established a system of selecting men for the Inspection Service who have already served in the Post Office Department for four years in some capacity, they have an unusual *esprit de corps*.

In some cases the maximum of four years is not demanded if the applicants substitute courses in accounting, law, engineering, or business administration for a part of this period.

Some knowledge of all these subjects is necessary in order to perform their job. In fact, the wider the range of the Postal Inspector's general knowledge, the more useful he will be.

One of the first pieces of advice given to a candidate for the service is: "Use your eyes." Whether on the job or off, he is expected to keep his eyes open, to observe people so clearly that he can describe them accurately, to notice the terrain around him, to acquaint himself with train and bus and airplane schedules and the best way to approach a given spot speedily and unobserved, to study the neighborhood that he may be in so that he knows something of the kind of people who live there.

When candidates for the Postal Inspection Service have been selected, they must pass a rigorous physical examination because a man has to be in peak condition and have sufficient energy to carry him through many hours of strenuous activity without a break. He must be between the ages of twenty-five and thirty-eight when he is appointed.

After taking a Civil Service examination he begins a seven-month program of academic and on-the-job training. His first month is classwork in the Washington, D.C., Bureau headquarters. Accompanied by an experienced man, he then has five months in actual field work. A final month back in Washington completes the schooling so that he is prepared to work as a full-fledged investigator.

He must learn something of self-defense and know how to restrain a violent suspect when the latter is arrested, as well as how to shoot if attacked by armed criminals. At the same time he discovers that it is not enough to be able to detect fraud or capture a criminal. He must learn how to interrogate a witness, how to present his findings in written form. He must know enough to marshal evidence that will stand up in court and to testify on the witness stand.

It is easy to see why the seven-month initial training is only the beginning. For the next two and a half years the program includes careful supervision of all work by a training counselor.

Along with tireless energy, the Postal Inspector has to have an inexhaustible supply of patience. There is an excitement about violent action that makes work stimulating. But non-action, the long, patient hours of waiting at a stake-out for the pay-off in blackmail or extortion cases, is harder to endure; in rain or cold, in crowded city streets or abandoned houses, hovering on a windy corner or behind a window or crouching behind a grave in a cemetery—he waits out the endless time. Is it worth it? The record shows that it is.

There is nothing haphazard about criminal investigation as it is practiced by the Postal Inspectors. They have, to help them substantiate or clarify their findings, all the resources of modern science, but the finding itself is up to them. They are taught the techniques of investigating everything from mailbox thefts to solving the incredible maze of mail frauds whose purpose is to cheat a gullible people of its money. They have to be crack shots and to master the dangerous and delicate job of rendering a bomb harmless, although today they are instructed to turn bombs over to agencies who have specialists to inactivate them.

And these represent only a small part of their activities. It is estimated that *Postal Inspectors make more than two hundred and fifty different kinds of investigations,* and from year to year new problems crop up. Secret Agents like Holbrook, in the early days of "the Ear Biters," devoted most of their time and energy to checking dishonesty within the post offices themselves or to protecting the mails from highwaymen. By the end of the Civil War, Special Agents like Parker had a new problem, riding with armed posses to protect the mails from gunmen or uncovering massive fraud schemes in which venal government officials and corrupt businessmen combined to cheat the Post Office Department.

Since 1900 these activities have broadened. The Postal Inspectors have had to combat the Black Hand in Chicago, the gangsters of the 1920s, and the mail frauds that increase daily, from fake lotteries to dishonest medical advertisements, from "get-rich-quick" schemes to "earn money at home" promises that are without foundation.

Of course, the five scientific laboratories are of the utmost value in providing special technical knowledge. The bulk of this work is done in connection with the analysis of handwriting to detect the writers of anonymous letters and to point out forgeries. Because of their exceptional resources and training, the laboratory experts are often called upon for their assistance by other agencies.

In the identification of fingerprints it is usually deemed essential to find twelve identical points to get a conviction in the federal court. With handwriting no specific number of points is required. But the bureau has gone much farther than the analysis of handwriting. It has, in co-ordination with the Bureau of Standards, developed a method of ink analysis so that the technicians can determine within minutes, by a single stroke of the pen, whether two inks are identical.

Criminals, aware that handwriting often betrayed them,

took to the typewriter. The bureau promptly countered by securing thousands of specimens of typewriter type going back as far as 1887, so that not only the make but the particular model of the machine can be identified.

Aside from the reward circulars, the quick eyes of 200,000 mail carriers, and the facilities of the laboratories, the Postal Inspectors have a lightning means of communication. This is the TWX, the Teletypewriter Exchange Call, by which a typewritten message can be sent from one office to another in seconds. By a "Conference Call," all the subscribers to the system can be united on a single hookup.

The value of this system was proved in a case involving a gang of money-order thieves. Stolen money orders are one of the chief objectives of mail thieves, because by careful forgery they can be cashed with comparative ease. In this case the local inspector got a description of the gang, the serial numbers of the stolen money orders, figured out where the thieves were probably going, and informed the other inspectors along the line by TWX. There was no opportunity for the forgers to cash in their stolen money orders. They were nabbed on the spot.

The training of the Postal Inspectors provides a remarkable course that covers a wide range of skills in detection.

Let's start with the way in which a Postal Inspector learns to trace a suspect. He does not, like Stephen Leacock's man on horseback, "ride off in all directions." His first job is to gather every bit of information he can about the suspect. No detail is too unimportant to be collected. A photograph in a high-school yearbook, a liking for a particular food, a slight mannerism, a trick of speech—all these seem too slight to matter. Each one of them has identified a number of criminals. So the inspectors learn not to overlook anything.

There is a story they tell about a wide search for a wanted man. Everyone knew that the fugitive must be in a certain small locality. He should be easy to find. People described his height, coloring, way of dress, age, general appearance. But one thing none of them mentioned. It was so obvious that it simply didn't occur to them that it was necessary to speak of it. The man had only one arm!

So the Postal Inspector compiles his data. He finds out the height of the wanted man, his probable weight, his coloring, his way of dressing. Then he gets down to details. How old does he appear to be? How does the man walk? Is he erect or slouching? Does he have a long stride or some peculiarity of movement? Actually we often recognize our friends on the street by their walk or carriage long before we can distinguish their faces.

Does the man have any peculiar gestures: pull at his ear, bite his nails, sniffle as though he had a perpetual cold? How does he talk? Does he have a foreign accent? Does he stutter? Does his speech indicate education or lack of it? Does he have a regional accent? A man from Maine and one from Missouri, one from Virginia, or one from Pennsylvania will speak in very different ways. Does he make use of any peculiar expressions?

The inspector checks to find out about the suspect's criminal record and *modus operandi,* for most habitual criminals tend to operate over and over in the same way. He checks the places at which he has worked in the past, his fellow employees, his friends and relations. Naturally he is most eager to get hold of fingerprints, a photograph, and a copy of the suspect's handwriting for a comparison.

Now, of course, life would be greatly simplified for the Postal Inspector if, after acquiring this information, he could rely on the suspect not changing his appearance. But he must also learn to study the arts and the many tricks of disguise so that he can recognize the suspect no matter what he has done to alter his looks.

Among the most common methods of disguise are dyeing or shaving the hair, cutting it in a different style, or growing a beard or mustache. The suspect may have the shape of his teeth altered. He may even go farther and have plastic surgery done to change the shape of nose or ears or eyelids. He may resort to an entirely different style of dress. In some extreme cases, by the use of tinted contact lenses, he appears to have changed the color of his eyes.

The trained detective learns to find leads that will give him a clue as to where his suspect has gone. Often such information is to be obtained from the public utilities companies that provide electric and gas and telephone service. From passport offices, steamship and railroad companies, bus or airplane lines, he may learn where he has gone. From motor vehicle bureaus and garages he may get a lead. The same thing applies to sources one might not think of: laundry and dry cleaning companies that have taken care of his clothes, hospitals in which he may have been a patient, tax bureaus, and even mailing lists. Of course, the man's past record is promptly checked with the police and with the FBI.

One of the most hackneyed situations in a detective story is the finding of an empty matchbook with the name of some hotel or motel, restaurant or night club. And yet a clue of this nature is constantly useful in tracing a suspect.

Once the suspect has been seen, the Postal Inspector has to know how to trail him without being observed or his presence suspected. If he is aware that he may be followed, the criminal will, of course, do everything he can to escape surveillance. He may change from one taxi to another, pick out a store or hotel with several entrances and try to escape his follower by using a different exit, mingle with a subway crowd at the rush hour and time his entrance to a subway train for the last second before the door closes.

It is because of these sudden demands on the ingenuity of the Postal Inspector, his need to make quick decisions, that the service requires its men to be in peak physical condition.

However, difficult as it often is to keep a suspect in sight when he is moving around, it is sometimes even more difficult to watch him when he decides to stay quietly in his own room or apartment. The Postal Inspector has to be able to see without being seen. What is he to do? Sometimes he sits in a parked car, pretending to read a newspaper. Sometimes he hides in a room across the street, watching the windows of the suspected person. Sometimes he finds a legitimate excuse for loitering by appearing to sweep the street or make a house-to-house canvass.

So far we have considered only the problems involved in identifying and watching the criminal himself. But what about the scene of the crime? Here, too, the Postal Inspector has to make use of all his powers of observation and to make an accurate and complete record of all the facts. That word *complete* means that he must not only know what the scene of the crime looked like; he must photograph and draw it and measure it carefully, including every article of furniture, the position of every fingerprint, the location of bullet holes, where a cigarette was found, even ascertaining the state of the weather at the time of the crime.

His next job is to learn how to question the suspect. This means that he must have some knowledge of psychology, know whether the people he is questioning are reliable or not, whether they are lying or merely uncertain, frightened or overimaginative, and how to deal with each individual case so as to get the best, the most accurate, the clearest story.

He must learn how to prepare a full and succinct report of all his findings. He must know enough law to be aware of what evidence must be produced in court and how it should be done. Finally, he has to be able to present that evidence in court in order to secure a conviction.

This, in brief, is an indication of the work that must be accomplished to solve a single case.

X ☆ More Lives than One

IN SOME WAYS it seems unfair to single out individuals in the Postal Service for special attention because almost all of them have amazing records. But Colonel William A. Kenyon is so good an example of the wide spread of activities of the Postal Inspectors that a little time will be taken to look at his career.

As has been pointed out, authorities estimate that these men perform some two hundred and fifty different kinds of investigations. In the case of Bill Kenyon, it seems as though he had to lead more lives than one in order to crowd in the variety of cases that fell to his lot.

He is, fortunately, another of the Postal Inspectors who has left some account of the incidents that occurred during the course of a crowded life. He was born in Charleston, South Carolina, and attended Porter Military Academy. While he was a student at Clemson College in Fort Hill, South Carolina, he needed a part-time job to eke out his expenses. He was paid ten cents an hour for emptying and stamping mail sacks for a small post office. Before he finished his career he was to become Assistant Chief Postal Inspector.

After serving in the Spanish-American War, Bill Kenyon

began delivering mail by way of a side-wheel steamer between Port Tampa and Havana. Transferred to the Philippine Postal Service, he was, in time, to make a complete circuit of the world.

In the early 1900s there were few trained government investigators. True, the Secret Service had started in 1860, but its duties were restricted to protecting the President of the United States and watching for counterfeiting activities. By 1908 the Federal Bureau of Investigation had started operation, but it did not function as it does now until 1924. During those early years, therefore, Postal Inspectors were often used by other government services for duties not only in the United States but around the world, drawing on their detective experience to cope with situations that had nothing to do with the mails.

During his busy lifetime Bill Kenyon has, at one time and another, been called on by other government departments for a variety of tasks, including the guarding and protection of a number of royal visitors.

In 1906 he was appointed inspector in New Orleans. At that time Louisiana was being plagued by safeblowers who wanted to lay hands on the great piles of silver dollars in the post office safes. Now silver dollars are considerably more cumbersome to handle than paper money, and sometimes the thieves had to bury their loot nearby, trusting that they could come back at a later time to retrieve it.

Bill Kenyon points out that in those days there was no quick method of sending out information about a wanted criminal and that the only way of pursuing him was by trains (which might run only once a day in small or isolated communities) or by horse and buggy.

One safeblower seemed to be operating with increasing success. Town after town reported that the post office safe had been blown and the money stolen. So Bill Kenyon started in pursuit. As usual, there were all sorts of descriptions that didn't fit and all sorts of rumors of the man having been seen which proved to be unfounded. Then Kenyon found his man, Matthew Griffen, and had him jailed at Shreveport.

Griffen, Kenyon related, was "a dapper, smooth-talking gent. The ladies visited him with baskets of food . . . In less than a week he had sawed his way out of jail, fled town, and mailed to the sheriff a poem." That poem, making fun of the whole pursuit, was the last straw. Kenyon recaptured his man and this time saw that he was sent to prison without any further receipt of baskets of food from his admiring friends and no concealed saw.

Like the mothers of too many habitual criminals, Griffen's mother simply refused to believe the charges against her son or the evidence that had been collected.

"He was always a good boy," she insisted.

To substantiate her belief, she had all the letters he had sent her, telling her how well he was doing as a steelworker on bridges, and sending her money from his "earnings." Those letters were of immense help to the prosecution. Invariably they had been mailed from towns where a safe had been blown.

One of Bill Kenyon's cases forced him to help a safeblower while he blew up a safe. It happened this way. Kenyon had been keeping an eye on a particular post office, knowing there was a good deal of money in the safe and that it was bound to provide a temptation to someone. He caught his man in the very act of blowing up the safe. But the man had gone so far that Kenyon dared not stop him. His primary job was to save government property, stamps and mail. So he told the safeblower to get on with the job.

Much to his amusement, the safeblower was extremely proud of his workmanship and he proceeded, greatly pleased at having such an audience. When the safe had been opened and the government property saved, Kenyon handcuffed his man and saw that he and his whole gang went to prison.

Then a Postal Inspector was wantonly murdered in Clinton, Mississippi. Inspector Charles Fitzgerald was old, kindly, and deeply respected. In the course of a routine check of the accounts of the post office at Clinton he found that they were short by $500. The assistant postmaster, a young man of twenty-two named William Sorsby, assumed that everyone was as crooked as he. He tried to bribe the elderly inspector, who refused. It was his job to protect the mails and see that the post office was honestly run.

The young man deliberately shot the inspector in the stomach, killing him. Kenyon took on the case. For three months he went over the town of Clinton with a fine-tooth comb, checking every street, every house, grimly determined that this brutal young killer should not escape. Meanwhile, as he knew, Sorsby's friends were keeping him concealed. At length he found the murderer hidden in an attic not far from the scene of his crime.

During those hectic years in the South, Kenyon came across the case of a man who went to incredible lengths to establish his innocence. People in a certain town began to receive anonymous letters that revealed a great deal of intimate knowledge of their personal affairs. They were wise enough to turn these over to the Postal Department. Kenyon read them. Only a family physician could know these facts about people, he decided. He talked to some of the victims and told them his suspicions. Their family doctor was So-and-So, the same man in every case. Yes, he could have known these things, but he simply could not be guilty; they all trusted him implicitly.

Kenyon secured a sample of the doctor's handwriting, which checked with the letters. He then confronted the doctor who denied the whole thing furiously. It was outrageous to suspect a man in his position.

Innocent as the doctor claimed to be, he began to carry a revolver, "for his own protection," he declared. Kenyon took good care to stay out of reach. But Postal Inspectors don't give up. As long as the doctor lived, he knew that there would be a man on his trail, trying to get the evidence that would put a stop to the career of this poison-pen writer.

Some time later the doctor's house was dynamited. Kenyon investigated and learned that the man had done it himself to prove that he was the innocent victim of persecution. Then the doctor was stabbed. Kenyon found out that he had done it with his own scalpel.

Finally one day a letter reached the Postal Inspector, a confession of writing the poison-pen letters. Kenyon checked on the author of the letter. He was an insane patient in a mental hospital. But, the hospital authorities said, in answer to his inquiry, the patient had disappeared. Shortly afterward his body was found in the woods, partly burned.

Kenyon began a meticulous examination of the scene. Tracks of sulky wheels were found near the body. The Postal Inspector checked and discovered that they matched the wheels of the doctor's sulky. He began to question people and at last found someone who had seen the doctor driving in his sulky on the night of the murder. There had been a large bundle propped up beside him.

The doctor was arrested, tried, and sentenced to life imprisonment.

In 1911 Bill Kenyon was transferred to the New York Post Office. A few years later he encountered one of those unforeseen problems that are not dramatic but are highly unpleasant. Melting snows caused a flood of the Hudson River in the Albany-Troy region. The floodwaters backed into the sewage system and there were three feet of water in the basement of the Troy post office. Somehow the stamps and stamped envelopes which had been stored there must be retrieved and accounted for, as they represented thousands of dollars.

After being soaked in water, the stuff was a solid mass, while the smell of wet cardboard and glue created such a stench that it was almost intolerable to breathe. Kenyon and his helpers managed to get out that soggy mass of smelly material, account for its value, and sell the whole thing to a pulp company. A disagreeable job, but it had to be done.

Then the Post Office Department came up with a new problem. Parcel post sent to Ecuador, Venezuela, Colombia, Peru, Chile, and Bolivia was suffering from so much theft that the situation had become intolerable. Kenyon was sent to South America to look into the situation, find out what the mail procedures were and where the weak spot lay.

The weak spot was easy to determine once he was on the spot. A half mile offshore parcel post was unloaded onto open barges and left unguarded. The thefts could not be chalked up to any one individual. It was the fault of an inefficient system. Everyone seemed to be helping himself. Not only the mail packages were taken but the very mail sacks were being used to make beds for the peasants. Kenyon saw children wearing American shoes, which they said they had bought at a bargain, as no doubt they had.

He set up a new system so that the mail would be protected by the proper checks and counterchecks, and the devastating loss of parcel-post packages in South America came to an end.

When the United States entered the First World War something had to be done to assure American soldiers of getting their mail. Bill Kenyon went to France and set up thirty APOs from one end of France to the other. But the problem remained unsolved. Men were shipped abroad with one division and then moved from place to place. Masses of undelivered mail began to stack up. There were, Kenyon pointed out, "28,137 Smiths, 26,999 Johnsons alone to add to the confusion." So a central post office was established at Bourges to clear all mail, and the soldiers could hear from their families at home without unreasonable delay.

Kenyon's most baffling case, he said, was that of the Spanish thefts. In 1919 and 1920 a number of American tourists in Spain spent a vast amount of money, which had been deposited there and was to be forwarded by registered mail to New York. But some fifty letters disappeared, containing at least $300,000.

Kenyon set off for Spain. To his great surprise, none of the Spanish officials had ever heard of the thefts. They knew nothing about them. Then he tried to trace the manner in which mail was handled, but the Spanish procedures were "so slipshod," he said, "that it was often impossible for me to trace the handling of a given letter."

At length he began to close in on the guilty men. One of them had stolen $65,000; another, $55,125; they had taken themselves off in a hurry. No one knew where they were to be found. Still another of the criminals had used his stolen money to set up what he called, with some sense of humor, the "American" salon of beauty. By this time the newspapers in Spain began to carry long accounts of the Spanish thefts, but the higher official still assured Kenyon that they had never heard of them, that they had no knowledge of the situation.

Finally, when Kenyon had gathered his evidence and was about to leave for home, he received a visitor. The man introduced himself as a lawyer for the thief who owned the "American" salon of beauty. Blandly he asked Kenyon how much he would give him if he helped recover what was left of the money or, he added, "suppressed evidence." He learned, as other men had learned before, that Postal Inspectors neither give nor accept bribes.

In the next few years Kenyon was called upon to act as escort and bodyguard for the Prince of Wales, Queen Marie of Romania, Prince Nobuco Asaka and Princess Yasuhito of Japan, Crown Prince Gustav and Crown Princess Louise of Sweden. When Prince Gustav wanted to take the famous mule trail down to the bottom of Grand Canyon, Kenyon, too, had to ride a mule and accompany the prince.

Later in his career Kenyon encountered the biggest stamp

thief America had produced, a man who made a clear profit of $3,000 a day. This man had developed a technique for removing cancellations from stamps by a secret process, for which he was arrested and served a year in prison. When he was released, he resumed his activities, this time working with a gang. He was a man of education, made an excellent personal impression, and addressed groups of philatelists most effectively. He built his business to such a scale that he was operating under ten different firm names.

At length Kenyon found his man, who was living in an attractive suite in a hotel. He took with him other Postal Inspectors, a supervisor for the post office, and a deputy United States Marshal. They introduced themselves as stamp dealers.

This was one of those fortunate circumstances where the criminal is literally caught in the act. On their arrival he was "laundering" stamps by his secret process to remove the cancellations. The men found over $800 in stamps in the room and, as Kenyon related jubilantly, "a truckload of evidence." Fortunately the criminal and his secret process went permanently out of circulation.

Bill Kenyon seemed to live more lives than one. When mail began to be carried on airplanes, it was his job to make every air flight to check on the average distance and the rates that should be established.

Then in 1937 Post Office Inspectors, with the co-operation of the Treasury and the War Department, supervised the transportation of gold bullion from New York and Philadelphia to Fort Knox. On the final trip alone there were over five thousand tons of gold, or $5,000,000,000.

"I have been asked," Bill Kenyon said, "how this immense wealth was insured. Uncle Sam carried the best insurance in the world—the steel bayonets of the United States Army and the integrity of the Postal Service. No better insurance exists."

XI ☆ They Fell for It

OVER THE COURSE of the years billions of dollars have been removed from the pockets of people who ought to know better, by means of the infinite number of ways that crooked individuals have discovered for using the mails to defraud. Most of us are familiar with stories of thefts which reach the newspapers because of some dramatic element, although the actual amount involved may be only a few hundred dollars. But year after year people allow themselves to be cheated of enormous amounts of money, often in swindles conceived and managed by men who have a position of some respectability in their community.

For a long time there was little the Postal Inspectors could do to prevent this wholesale rooking of the people. Immigrants, coming to America and ignorant of its customs, were preyed upon by these unscrupulous con men. In later years it began to seem that people of all degrees of education and experience were equally gullible. The most fantastic claims that promised easy money without work, improved health without doctors, a successful career in the arts without talent—there was no type of fraud that did not find someone not only willing but eager to believe in it.

In 1872 federal laws on the statute books made it a penal offense to use the mails to defraud, and at last the Postal Inspectors were able to move in on the grafters, to expose their activities, and to put them out of business.

Among these general fields of mail fraud are:

a) medical advertising of drugs or appliances that are not only worthless but often actually dangerous;

b) get-rich-quick lotteries;

c) courses on how to be a detective by mail, all the promises to publish books or songs or provide education and, ugliest of all, the "earn money at home" swindle;

d) the inheritance racket;

e) the catch-penny devices.

These represent only a few of the main categories of "F" (fraud) cases by which the American people have permitted themselves to be cheated. Of course, it is impossible to know how much money has actually been obtained in this way. A number of victims refuse to admit that they permitted themselves to be gulled. Some kinds of fraud take years to be exposed. But certainly, in the twenty-five years between 1900 and 1925, at least $100,000,000 went into the pockets of swindlers, extracted from people who refused to learn by experience and continued to believe that, by some magic, they could get something for nothing. In the eight years between 1934 and 1942, $661,580,000 went into fraudulent mail-order schemes. In the field of medical fraud the money has soared to billions.

Something of the extent of this type of fraud becomes evident when we learn that postal authorities firmly believe that sales of fake oil stocks became so prevalent between 1919 and 1929 that they played a great part in producing the Wall Street crash of 1929 and the Great Depression.

Even after a federal law was passed making it a crime to use the mails to defraud, Postal Inspectors had trouble in bringing a case to court and getting a conviction. The defense would claim that the advertisement or letter sent out by the swindler indicated no intention whatsoever to be dishonest. A Postal Inspector named Joe P. Johnston, who later became chief of the service, was determined to put a stop to these frauds and to clarify the ruling so that the swindlers could no longer escape the law. His opportunity came in what was a rather trivial case.

A dishonest Arkansas postmaster advertised: "Counterfeit? No! Confederate $20.00 sample bill sent by mail for $2.00."

Before long, so many people had sent in two dollars that the postmaster was coining money. Johnston said that the advertisement was so worded as to make people believe they were really getting counterfeit $20 bills.

No one was particularly anxious to prosecute the case because it looked as though the postmaster had an excellent chance of succeeding with it. So Johnson handled it himself. By the time he had finished his argument, Judge Shires told the jury that a defendant was liable for what he *intended* his victims to believe, not for the actual wording of an advertisement. Johnston won his case and the postmaster was convicted of using the mails to defraud.

A real beginning had been made. Now the Inspection Service had the strong weapon of the law on its side. Johnston immediately set to work to clean up other examples of the same type of fraudulent advertising and so brought to an end a long series of crimes.

For some reason Kansas seemed to be a favorite area for the operation of fraud schemes. Indeed, the Midwest has always been a particularly lucrative source of income to charlatans. In the early years of this century advertisements began to appear offering a course in "How To Be a Detective by Mail." The cost of the course was ten dollars, and when it was completed the "student" would receive a tin badge.

Thousands of young people assumed that, armed with the tin badge, they would at once get jobs as detectives and be in a position to earn a great deal of money. Indeed, the advertisements claimed that detectives were in demand everywhere.

Johnston set out to put a stop to this swindle. He took the matter up with the United States District Attorney. The latter refused to have any part in it. His argument was that, after all, the people who subscribed to the detective course received lessons by mail and got a badge. Who could prove dishonest intent?

Johnston felt that he could—and he did. He presented the case in court himself and got the convictions he was after. Since then thousands of similar frauds have been stopped and punished as a result of Johnston's work and his grim determination to bring an end to this preying on the public.

Not, of course, that the time ever comes when the Postal Inspectors feel that they have put an end to mail fraud. As they unearth one and eliminate it, another arises. In fact, the Washington Bureau of the Postal Inspection Service has over a quarter of a million cards, indicating people and firms that have taken part in mail frauds. Often when one company is closed up the same people start business again under another name, so a careful and unceasing watch is kept for these recurrent cases.

Most dangerous of all forms of mail fraud is the field of the medical quack. Of all the rackets in the United States it is this, and not, as one might suppose, the more noisy activities of robbers and gangsters, that brings in the most money, hundreds of millions of dollars every single year. Indeed, of the five to twenty-five billion dollars that goes into the pockets of criminals yearly, most of it is pocketed by racketeers who are not regarded as swindlers at all by many of the people who know them.

A certain number of periodicals do not bother to check the validity of the concerns that advertise in their pages, so the Postal Inspectors have added to their enormous number of responsibilities that of investigating medical advertising. Often, under assumed names and from fake addresses, Postal Inspectors write for the products advertised. These are turned over to other agencies specializing in chemistry, anatomy, therapeutics, and bacteriology, who are prepared to analyze the products and indicate whether they are valid or worthless. Some of these ugly methods of preying on the health and well-being of the people have brought in the staggering total of $225,000 a day.

As far as possible the Postal Inspectors continue to warn the public not to deal with unauthorized sources, particularly where their health is concerned, but there are too many credulous individuals who will fall for any suggestion, no matter how absurd it may be, that seems to promise them health and youth and eternal beauty. When such products promise cures for cancer, tuberculosis, and other serious conditions, the authorities have to be alert to stop their distribution. And yet, when proof of worthlessness and even harm is established, some of the victims who still persist in believing in magical remedies continue to think that these prescriptions and therapeutic devices really work and do them good.

One of the corrupt operators, perhaps the most successful of them all, made so much money out of the public that he was able to publish a newspaper, to run radio stations and even hospitals. The fact that many of his "patients" died under his cures did not upset or deter him in the least.

As a result of constant vigilance the Postal Inspectors are able to check the activities of nearly 60 per cent of these medical frauds and to make their perpetrators sign stipulations of discontinuance. But the rest often emerge under new names with new products, new cures, and there are always people who believe in them because they want to believe in the impossible.

How many times have all of us seen bald barbers selling cures for baldness and watched a credulous man pay for this miraculous stuff, even after he has had a good look at the barber's bald head.

Get-rich-quick is an appeal that seems to meet with a constant response from gullible people. The worst of it is that, no matter how often they are fooled, they seem to believe that next time they will really find the pot of gold at the end of the rainbow.

The easiest and most irresistible appeal to such people is the lottery. The truth is that the overwhelming number of lottery tickets sold in the United States, perhaps 90 per cent of them, whether representing American or foreign lotteries, are either based on nonexistent lotteries or are forgeries of the real ones. In other words, they are worthless. And yet from one to five billion dollars a year are paid out by people who can ill afford it for these worthless bits of paper which, in their eyes, are golden keys to fortune.

Kansas City, in 1935, was the center of a huge lottery swindle, which purported to be sponsored by a military hospital. It would be interesting to learn how many people donate money for churches, hospitals, research in various diseases, crippled children, which never see the money, and without troubling to find out whether they are the real thing. The Postal Inspectors, alerted to the situation, moved in and drifted around town, looking in the most likely places for evidence that lottery tickets were being sold. In a cigar store they found a book of tickets; this was supposed to be a lottery on the Kentucky Derby, with a first prize of $100,000.

"I don't know the man who left the book here," the cigar-store owner said. "There were twelve tickets in it and he said if I sold ten of them at $1 each, I could keep two of them for myself." The chance of winning $100,000 for $1! That was the irresistible bait, and the fish rose obligingly to take it.

With a federal statute on mail fraud the operators had begun to have a healthy fear of using the mails. The inspectors knew that a man who had been convicted of using the mails to defraud and had been released from prison was said to be in Kansas City. Probably he was up to his old tricks. For criminals, like their victims, often fail to learn by their mistakes. Each time they hope that they'll get away with it, even if they failed before.

All mail carriers were instructed to report any tenant in any office building who received no mail at all. Such a case in itself would be suspicious. Two days later a report came in. A certain mercantile company had never got a single letter.

The inspectors called upon the rental agent. Yes, a man had rented two rooms in his building for this company.

"What is his name?"

"He didn't give his name," the agent said, "but he paid the rent in cash, so I thought it was all right."

What did he know about his tenant?

He knew nothing at all, the agent admitted. The locks had been changed after the tenant moved in and he had refused to have janitor and cleaning service, which meant that no building employee had been inside the rooms since they had been rented.

The inspectors were greatly interested in this discreet and retiring tenant. They went up to take a look at the rooms for themselves. As they had expected, the doors were locked and, in addition to that, the hall windows, letter slot, even the keyhole had been covered on the inside to prevent anyone from seeing what went on.

The inspectors, through a small hole in the paper that covered a window, were able to look in. They saw cardboard cartons piled all over the rooms. They then called the police and, with their authorization, raided the premises. They found all the evidence they needed, nearly a ton and a half of lottery tickets. The only trouble was that their man had vanished. Apparently someone had told him that the Postal Inspectors were closing in.

They did find one clue, however, a white felt hat with the initials J. B. Apparently they had been right. These were the criminal's initials. Under a new firm name he had gone back to his business of peddling fake lottery tickets.

There was no telling where he had gone or what name he was hiding behind. The next obvious step was to find the engraving company that had made the plates for the fake lottery tickets. This was done and the owner of the company admitted that he had made the plates for the fake lottery tickets. He broke down and told them where to find their man, who was living in a nearby hotel. In his trunk they found mailing lists of prospective victims. They had all the evidence they needed for a conviction.

Allied to the lottery ticket racket is the favorite swindle of selling stock in nonexistent gold mines or oil wells. Curiously enough, it is not simply the ignorant or the naïve who fall for this type of fraud. A number of industrialists, members of Chambers of Commerce, Boards of Trade, even the Stock Exchange—the list is legion of people who, in spite of hardheaded experience, fall for the lure of something for nothing. Incredibly enough, these men succumb not once but over and over to the same swindlers for the same kind of swindle!

One of the most successful gangs peddling fake stocks persuaded a rich industrialist to invest $100,000 in a company. He lost everything. Then they went back to see their victim. Was the latter suspicious? Not at all.

Because the man had lost so much money one of the gang told him that he wanted to compensate by making him his heir. He had willed the industrialist all his rights to patents in radio, television, and electronics. Sixty million dollars could be gained easily from the movie and television firms that had been infringing on these patents. But, of course, it would take some cash to buy releases from the other stockholders.

So the industrialist began to put up more money. In the long run he turned over $423,771 to the swindler. By that time his brokers insisted on making an investigation. They turned over the information they had gathered to Postal Inspector C. A. Miller of Rochester. Miller went back over the files on mail frauds. There he found the swindler's record, compiled by the late Inspector Herb Graham. In his time Graham had arrested more fraud operators than any other man in the United States and had become known to the swindlers as "Mr. Poison" and "Mr. Nemesis."

So the swindler was arrested, convicted, and sent to prison. And the industrialist? Well, it's just possible that he turned an attentive ear to the next plausible con man who came up with a get-rich-quick idea.

XII ☆ The Inheritance Swindle and "The Great I Am"

THERE IS hardly any area of human activity in which an astute swindler does not try to make easy money at the expense of the public. Some of these schemes are trivial; some of them are far-reaching and dangerous. Yet it is difficult to persuade the public, even after it has once been cheated, that it is wise to think twice before accepting at face value any offers and promises that may be made. The same people persist over and over in throwing good money after bad in the hope that, sooner or later, the gamble will pay off. Of course, it doesn't.

Among the sillier examples are the following:

An advertisement for a way to exterminate potato bugs brought a lot of responses. Here's what the farmers received for their money: "Catch the bug, put him between two boards, and mash him."

Another advertisement asked people to send 25¢ for a coat hanger. What they received was a nail. Advertisements of a steel engraving of George Washington—$1, please—brought a 1¢ stamp. Another one said, "Send 10¢ and learn something valuable." For once they did. "Do not answer advertising of this kind," came the mocking response.

In some of these rackets the guilty people were discovered simply because they did not use the mails. How then can the Postal Inspectors get a conviction on the mail-fraud statute? Because, whether or not the swindler uses the mails himself, it is almost impossible for him to operate without someone using the mails; say, a victim who has written to him about his fake product or whatever it may be. If he receives so much as a check or a postcard through the mails he comes under the jurisdiction of the Post Office Department. And so far the swindlers have found considerable difficulty in receiving money unless the victims send checks at one time or another.

While one may not feel much sympathy for people who get cheated because they want something for nothing, there is another group of people who are being cheated year in and year out, a defenseless group that can ill afford the money that is taken from them by fake mail-order schemes. These are the people with little money, or those whose health requires them to remain at home and who seek some education by mail, a chance to publish books and songs, and especially to "earn money at home."

Something like five hundred million dollars a year is taken from these miserable people, and often the companies that are growing rich out of this contemptible exploitation of need are made up of men who stand high in the social life of their cities.

Fake literary agencies advertise that, for a small sum, they can place a book and make a fortune for the writer. Now, as a general rule, good publishers do not advertise for scripts and sound literary agents do not earn money directly from their clients. They take a percentage of the money they earn for them. But countless people, without training or talent, are easily led to believe that they can produce masterpieces.

One example of this was a man who advertised that he would review and criticize songs, have records made by noted artists, and fame would be waiting on the doorstep. What really happened was that the enterprising young man who ran this particular racket would sing the song himself while his office girl played the accompaniment. The delighted song writer would receive the record and wait for eager offers from the music publishers. That, of course, was the end of it.

To stimulate interest the swindler advertised a song contest. He claimed that prizes amounting to large sums had been given to the winners. The Postal Inspectors got the names of the two winners, looked them up, and discovered without surprise that they had not written songs, had never heard of such a contest and, naturally, had received no prize money. The young man went to jail.

Over and over efforts are made to put an end to the fake literary agents who, for a small sum, promise to turn the amateur's book into an enormous financial success. In one instance a Postal Inspector tried them out. He wrote the worst book he could manage, ill-spelled, ungrammatical, and filled with utter nonsense about a quite imaginary journey. In reply he got a letter asking him to pay for the proper criticism and help, because the agent saw in the script "elements of primitive strength and hidden beauty."

Another fraud order was issued and another fake agent went out of circulation.

The "earn-money-at-home" swindle preys on the sick and the elderly and the impoverished. A typical example of this was a show-card company of Toronto, Canada. This organization advertised that people could earn from $15 to $60 a week at home in spare time by making show cards. The concern had grown to such dimensions on the basis of its false claims that it could afford to advertise in twenty-nine national magazines and newspapers.

For years a Postal Inspector followed up this company, investigating, trying to force it out of business. When he went to Canada, the local postal men there were horrified. They took the American investigator for a drive to look at the impressive homes owned by the heads of the concern; they pointed out that these men were church members and community leaders.

The Postal Inspector was not impressed by what the heads of the concern had spent their money for; what interested him was how they had earned it. A follow-up was made of over six thousand people who had put money into the scheme by which they hoped to learn to make show cards and earn money at home. They found exactly sixty-seven Canadians and thirty-six Americans out of the whole lot who were actually able to earn money out of the scheme. The others, ranging from the crippled, the impoverished, the elderly, and the very young, had put in their money and got nothing in return.

Finally pressure from the Postal Department became so insistent that the Solicitor General of the Post Office Department in Washington required the heads of the racket to prove that their advertisements were honest and that their subscribers were not being cheated.

They agreed. They appeared with twenty-nine suitcases of documents and an array of legal talent. Against all this imposing evidence and a battery of defense attorneys the American Postal Inspector stood alone. His heart sank. This time they were going to get away with it.

Then, to open their case impressively, they brought out a contract for $1,000,000 for show cards to be produced for the Sappho Company. This seemed to clinch the matter almost before the hearing had begun. Then, quietly, the Postal Inspector reached into his brief case and pulled out a short report. The Sappho Company had gone into bankruptcy. The contract was valueless.

At last the heads of the show-card company were forced to sign a stipulation that they would no longer teach show-card making by mail. They got thirty days to shut up shop.

One of the strangest cases, because it represented clearly that, however sure the proof, a number of people would prefer to be defrauded, was the Sir Francis Drake inheritance racket, by which an unsophisticated farm boy managed to collect well over a million dollars from some forty thousand people who, many of them having been cheated repeatedly, were ready and eager to come back for more.

Back in the early days of the present century a farm woman in Iowa fell for a smooth-talking swindler who told her that she was the heir to a great estate but that she would have to invest some money for the legal work that would be necessary to prove her claim. Of course, once he had his hands on the woman's savings, the man disappeared and she heard no more of this great inheritance.

Her son brooded about the matter. Ignorant, unpolished,

apparently a harmless and uncouth farm boy, he began to think about his mother's loss. It occurred to him that, after all, if she had fallen for such a racket, there must be a lot of other people who would do the same thing.

With the help of two partners the son formed the Sir Francis Drake Association. Drake, of course, had died in 1596. The idea the three swindlers dreamed up was that the Drake property, with the accumulated interest of over three hundred years, would now amount to "a conservative twenty-two billion dollars."

The original plan was to find some man named Drake. They did. Ernest Drake was greatly interested and he invested money in the scheme.

The two partners gave up after the first successful attempt, but the farm boy had more vision. If one Drake would participate in the great inheritance scheme, why not other Drakes? Why not all the Drakes who could be unearthed?

Why not, indeed? The Drakes of the United States and Canada went along eagerly. At first each one put up a few dollars as a member of the Sir Francis Drake Association, all of them to share in the final division of the colossal estate.

Then it began to appear that, while the young man had been assigned the control of the fortune and its final distribution, the job was going to prove an expensive one and more money would be needed. And, of course, the greater the sum invested, the larger the percentage of the estate one would get.

As time went on, year after year, a few of the less credulous investors began to balk at putting up any more money; they wanted, belatedly, to see some credentials from the promoter. So the Postal Inspectors appeared on the scene. They discovered that, while a few of the victims were willing to talk, a number were not. Either they still had hopes of collecting a vast fortune or they were embarrassed at having been played for suckers.

The Postal Inspectors then consulted the manager of the American Express Company in London where the former plowboy was living, apparently engrossed in coping with the vast Drake estate. They wanted to know whether he had been receiving an unusual amount of money from the United States. He had indeed, the manager assured them. Between 1924 and 1933 he had received some $730,000 through the American Express Company.

Then the facts began to come out. He had, over that ten-year period, been receiving larger and larger sums from his victims, ranging from $15,000 to $35,000, while one woman had donated over $100,000 to the cause.

By this time the Postal Inspectors had drawn up a list of more than forty thousand people who had contributed to the Sir Francis Drake scheme. (Later they were to find an improved and enlarged list of seventy thousand names.) The promoter was deported from England as an undesirable alien and met by grim-faced Postal Inspectors when he arrived in New York. It was estimated that he had taken over $1,250,000 from his victims.

The case came to trial. The Postal Inspectors had made sure that the promoter's men stopped making collections, but the victims themselves simply refused to believe that they had been cheated. Even when the promoter was sentenced to ten years in the penitentiary and the whole ugly story was made public, their faith in him and in that twenty-two-billion-dollar fortune was unshaken. People who had paid over and over again now mortgaged their farms and sent their last penny to help with the defense of the man who had cold-bloodedly robbed them. He left behind him a monument of human wreckage: penniless people, empty savings accounts, foreclosed farms. One woman could not go to court to testify until someone lent her a dress. She had given the swindler everything she had.

It was not, however, farmers alone who were the victims of this preposterous inheritance scheme. Among those who appeared in court—and testified for the defense!—were a member of the Chamber of Commerce in North Dakota and a member of the Board of Trade in Chicago.

Of all the incredible kinds of fraud by mail, perhaps the ugliest was one that capitalized not on people's greed, vanity, or desire for marvelous cures but on their fear of sickness and death and instead promised its followers immortality.

Under a number of aliases a certain individual had spent his early years selling fake gold shares. While he was hiding from the law he began to read books on the occult in his sister-in-law's bookshop. This, he decided, should prove to be a gold mine.

With his wife, who formerly had played in vaudeville, and his son, he headed for California, where he launched his new career. He started by writing a book. According to its author, he could help anyone to conquer "misery, poverty, disease and death."

The book made a great hit and money began to pour in. The author then built a temple where he held classes in his new cult. So many people came flocking to the temple to hear his teachings that he held classes all day long, seven days a week. The money was gushing in now like a newly tapped oil well. In time he had enough to buy a press for himself to print his book; he ran a monthly magazine and even bought extensive radio time.

Seeing how easy people were to exploit, he then began to manufacture rings and pins and pictures that were symbolic of the new religion, and these, too, were snatched up like hot cakes. Apparently there was no end to what people would fall for.

As long as his followers were so anxious to give him their money, this cult leader told them that they ought to make "love gifts" to their new saint. Did it work? Of course it did. People sent in over $100,000 as well as pieces of treasured family jewelry.

He was now well into his stride. There were over three hundred branches of his new religion, more than half a million members. What could he do next? People paid for his lectures, for his book, for the rings and pins and pictures he had for sale; they obediently sent him "love gifts." Well, he might as well make a really big coup. He'd ask them to give everything they had to the new cult. The end of the world was in sight and, after all, they wouldn't get any good out of their money anyhow.

So he had set up a foundation and so far he had managed to pay no taxes at all on the money he had been raking in. Then the unexpected happened. The one who promised his followers freedom from disease and death, died in a hospital. At first his wife and son did everything they could to keep people from knowing what had happened. In spite of all their efforts the secret was made public. Mother and son did some quick thinking. They informed their followers that, in accordance with their teachings, their leader had made his ascension.

Meanwhile some of the followers had grown restive; they had begun to realize how preposterous the temple and the teachings were. So reports began to come into the Post Office Department. The foundation was using the mails to defraud.

Two inspectors, W. F. Callahan and J. H. Van Meter, began to investigate the mail-fraud element of the outfit. They not only studied the letters and publications that had been sent through the mails, but they began to interview people who had lost their fervor and withdrawn from the group. In time they talked with nearly two hundred of them, and the evidence was piling up. They turned then to the widow and her son and over twenty members of the staff. Next thing they knew, the leaders of the cult were charged with mail fraud and given a hearing by a federal grand jury. After a bitterly fought trial they were found guilty.

To add to their grief, the Treasury Department became interested in the foundation. What? All this income and no taxes?

"But those were love gifts," they explained. "You can't ask us to pay taxes on love gifts."

The Internal Revenue Bureau did not agree. They got $104,943.63 in back taxes and penalties.

Year in and year out the Postal Inspectors continue tirelessly running to ground the people who are guilty of mail frauds. And, year after year, they continue to hope that some day people will check with their local post office when they receive dubious offers through the mail, whether lotteries are involved or stocks or promises of health and wealth and success. They hope that the person receiving an anonymous or threatening letter will not cravenly pay up but that he will leave it to the Postal Inspectors. For the Postal Inspectors get their men and the individual must have no further fears.

XIII ☆ The Train Robbers

TRAIN NUMBER THIRTEEN of the Southern Pacific was an express between San Francisco, California, and Portland, Oregon. At noon on an October day in 1923, Number Thirteen was nearly at the entrance to a tunnel. As it slowed up, several men who had been lurking at the side of the tracks leaped into the cab and ordered the engineer to stop the train. Because they were armed he did so.

Then the engineer and fireman were told to get off. They climbed down from the cab and stood with their hands high above their heads, helpless to do anything else.

The mail clerk, wondering why the train had stopped, stuck out his head from the door of the mail car. A barrage of gunfire met him and he jumped back inside and locked the door.

A few moments later the passengers on the train heard so tremendous an explosion that they thought the engine had blown up. When they got out to investigate they found that a blasting machine had been placed under the end of the mail car. The robbers had misjudged the amount of force necessary, so instead of making an opening in the car, they had wrecked it entirely, killing not only the mail clerk inside but a brakeman who had been close to the car at the time of the disaster, trying to find out what was wrong.

The horrified passengers then discovered that both the engineer and the fireman had been shot down in cold blood because they were the only ones who had seen the bandits' faces.

That was the story of the Oregon holdup. The mail robbers had gained nothing because they had completely destroyed the mail sacks they had intended to rob, and they had left behind them the dead bodies of four men.

At once Postal Inspectors were called in to solve the case and to track down the killers. As there was not a single living eyewitness, they began a slow and patient search for clues. The only evidence they found near the wrecked train was a .45 caliber Colt automatic. Only the last two figures of the serial number remained, the rest having been laboriously removed.

Slowly the inspectors widened their search. The scene of the crime had nothing left to offer them, but the men had come from somewhere. The crime had been carefully thought out, even though it had been badly botched at the end.

About a mile away they found six footpads made out of gunnysack to prevent leaving footprints. Six footpads meant three men. At the same spot they found a blasting machine and a pair of overalls. The overalls seemed to have no particular points of interest, but they did not know what a laboratory might find, so they took them along.

At length the investigators came to a deserted mountain camp. From indications inside they decided that three men had occupied it for at least several days. This must have been the hide-out of the mail bandits. The mountain camp provided no other information. Apparently the men had been careful to remove all clues or fingerprints. That left only the pair of overalls. They didn't seem to be of much use except that there appeared to be grease stains on them.

Grease. That might indicate that the wearer of the overalls had worked in a garage. This interested the Postal Inspectors particularly because, in a town not far off, there was a garage mechanic who was an ex-convict. Perhaps he had failed to learn by his experience and he had broken the law again.

Postal Inspectors, however, are trained to keep an open mind and not to make snap judgments. They must have evidence to back them up. So, instead of questioning the mechanic, they sent the overalls to Professor E. C. Heinrich, a criminologist of the University of California. It was time to learn what a scientific laboratory could turn up.

Professor Heinrich examined the "grease" on the overalls and analyzed the microscopic dust in the pockets. The stain, he reported, was not grease; it was pitch from Douglas fir trees. The evidence of the overalls indicated a lumberjack, not a mechanic.

Then he came to his most important finding. In a small pocket he had discovered a tiny fragment of paper. Carefully reconstructed by the laboratory, it proved to be a receipt for a registered parcel, which had been mailed from Eugene, Oregon, by Roy De Autremont.

The jubilant Postal Inspectors now had something concrete to work on: they knew the name of one of the three bandits and a place where he had stayed. At Eugene they added to their information. Roy was one of three De Autremont brothers; he had a twin named Ray and a younger brother Hugh.

So the pursuit got under way. At Albany the inspectors found the store in which Roy had bought the Colt automatic that he had lost at the scene of the attempted train robbery. In Portland they found the shop where the brothers had bought a car.

Now all the training in the art of tracing suspects began to pay off. Little by little the inspectors built up a clear picture of the three brothers. They knew their habits and their interests. They found out that the twins had to wear glasses and got hold of the prescription for their glasses; they even learned exactly what dental work they had had done.

They discovered that Hugh was a reader who often visited public libraries. He seemed to have a special liking for books about Jesse James. As the brothers were too young to be inducted into the First World War—they were only seventeen at the time the United States entered the war—they had got jobs in lumber camps, where they were greatly impressed by revolutionary ideas. Roy organized the I.W.W. and Ray spent a year in the Washington State Reformatory. There the Postal Inspectors added his fingerprints to their physical data on the crime.

The cold-blooded murder of the four men had aroused the Post Office Department. Postal Inspector F. Tennyson Jefferson was instructed to stick to the case until he solved it, if it took the rest of his life.

All in all, it was to take three and a half years and to cost more than $500,000 to solve the case. Jefferson, answering countless tips, followed the men patiently from place to place. Every resource of the Post Office Department was used to uncover the three young bandits. WANTED circulars, more than two million of them, were printed in a number of languages and distributed not only in post offices but in police stations, employment centers, recruiting stations, railroad stations. They also went to barbers, dentists, oculists, and the libraries Hugh enjoyed so much. Slowly the net was tightening, with an incentive in the form of rewards of $19,500 to encourage prompt reports on the whereabouts of the bandits.

Postal Inspectors are dedicated men who do not seek personal publicity, but they welcome all the publicity they can get about the men they are seeking. Sooner or later someone would recognize the pictures of the wanted men.

Jefferson, undeterred by many disappointments, continued to follow up every tip, even when they seemed fantastic, even when they came from foreign countries. Such a search engenders an excitement of its own in the beginning, but when month follows month, and year after year drags on, it is difficult to keep up the same enthusiasm.

More than three years after the blasting machine blew up the mail car of Train Number Thirteen outside an Oregon tunnel, a young man sauntered into the San Francisco post office. Idly he glanced at the WANTED posters. He turned back to one that looked familiar. That man had served with him in the United States Army in the Philippines.

Jefferson was informed at once. Yes, the young soldier assured him, he was sure of his identification. So a Postal Inspector took passage on a ship for Manila. There he found Hugh De Autremont, whom he brought back under arrest.

Then one Sunday a reader of a newspaper special article about the three-year-old crime studied the photographs. Two years before, men who looked like the twins Roy and Ray had lived at Steubenville, Ohio. So once more Jefferson was on his way, this time to Steubenville, where he found the other two bandits. The three brothers were tried and sentenced to life imprisonment.

At last Postal Inspector Jefferson was free to turn his attention to other matters.

Bill Fahy was one of the most successful of the Postal Inspectors. After serving in Philadelphia for several years he asked for a transfer, in 1919, to the Chicago Division, where he would have a wider opportunity to show his abilities.

Within a comparatively short time he had made good use of his opportunities. In those years mail robberies were becoming more common in the Chicago area, and Fahy soon proved that he could solve even the toughest cases. For the next five years he helped to solve every big mail robbery and he became known as the most brilliant inspector in the district.

Fahy seemed to know just how to deal with gangs, however violent they might be, and to get any help or information he needed from the underworld. He had a confident manner that grew more confident as he became more spectacularly successful. Slim and well dressed, he aroused a great deal of admiration in his colleagues. No one else was able to get the same collaboration from the Chicago underworld; no one else got so many tips about crimes that were being planned; no one else knew where to lay hands on wanted men.

Fahy had taken great trouble in establishing his underworld contacts. He found that if he were friendly toward the people who kept involving themselves in crime, if he arranged for light sentences wherever it was possible, he acquired a source of information that was invaluable to him.

The problem with this kind of association was that it might easily work both ways. For a few years Fahy held out a helping hand and tried to protect the men who brought him information. Then slowly, almost imperceptibly, the situation changed. The criminals with whom he dealt were not always either stupid or incompetent. It occurred to some of them that it might be well to cultivate the engaging and brilliant young Postal Inspector.

At that time the head of a big and powerful bootleg liquor gang was James Murray, who was an important figure in Chicago politics. He also had a side line as a fence, handling stolen property. Murray had no difficulty in selling his beer and rum, but it was not always easy to transport it. The police had an unpleasant habit of keeping an eye on trucks that might be used for bootlegging.

Murray took his time establishing a friendship with Fahy. When he felt the time was ripe, he pointed out that there was some easy money to be made by escorting a truck loaded with beer and rum. With Fahy on the truck no other law-enforcement officer would dream of stopping it.

So Fahy, the only Postal Inspector ever to be faithless to his trust, looked at the money Murray offered him and accepted the deal. Meantime, though he was spending more money than he could possibly earn on his salary, his record in running down mail thieves was so brilliant that no one suspected him of wrongdoing.

Then Fahy's life grew more complicated, as it was bound to do. Being involved in Chicago politics and Chicago rackets, he took a strong dislike to "Big Tim" Murphy, a Chicago politician, and decided to railroad him to prison. In 1921 the mail room of the Dearborn Street Station was robbed of $329,000 in Liberty bonds and $59,000 in cash. Fahy promptly caught four of the bandits and had them arrested. The fifth escaped but was caught, eleven years later, and sent to prison.

By this time Fahy was beginning to show his true colors. He offered the four men whom he had arrested light sentences if they would say Murphy was involved in the deal. So they did, and Fahy got rid of an enemy.

All this time Fahy had kept up his association with Murray, who was invaluable at getting rid of stolen property and securities and pointing out opportunities for big robberies.

So far, while Fahy had been adding steadily to his income by protecting trucks of bootleg liquor, he had not really got into the big money. Then one day in 1924 Murray began to assemble some of his gangster friends: Brent Glasscock, a Kansas City gunman; the four Newton brothers, Jess, Joe, Willis, and Willie, Texas bank robbers; and Herbert Holliday of Little Rock, Arkansas.

Murray told his friends that he was calling them in for a big operation, a mail-truck robbery. A lot of money would be involved. So the men met for lunch at a restaurant in the Loop and Murray appeared, bringing with him his friend Bill Fahy, Postal Inspector, who was prepared to be the finger man of a big holdup.

They asked what he had in mind. He said that there was a $100,000 payroll that went to Indiana twice a month. He could tell them when and where. To Fahy that sounded like a lot of money. But the gangsters thought it over, considered the risk, mentally divided the loot among them all, and decided that it wasn't worth while.

"Well," Fahy said slowly, "the biggest possible haul is Train Number Fifty-seven of the Chicago, Milwaukee and St. Paul Railroad."

A train robbery. That was much more risky. The men hesitated.

"The register pouches alone contain millions," Fahy told them. "That train carries nothing but mail."

Millions! That was more like it. The gangsters were really interested by this time. Then Fahy took charge. He knew better than any of them, from long years of experience, that the punishment for armed robbery of the mails is a fixed sentence of twenty-five years from which there is no escape. He had sent a number of men to that punishment himself. He knew how the Postal Inspectors worked, how tenacious they were in following up mail robbery, what routine they followed.

Still, he had proved to be the most brilliant and effective investigator in his area. He was sure he could cope with the system. Only, and he made this point clear, he was the man who knew the job, who knew what steps the Postal Service would take, who knew exactly how great the risks would be. They were to leave the organization of the crime to him; they were to accept his orders as final. If they did exactly what he told them, he would be in full charge of the investigation and all would go well.

"You'll be investigating your own crime," Glasscock told him in amusement.

Fahy was not amused. He set to work to plan the perfect crime. Nothing was to be left to chance. He told them when and how to board the train. He explained that the mail clerks would never open the locked doors of their cars if it were attacked. The best thing to do would be to break the windows by shooting at them and then fill the cars with poison gas.

The men set about buying rifles, shotguns, revolvers, formaldehyde, and gas masks. Fahy told them where the robbery must take place, a spot where there were a number of good roads. They must get hold of four stolen cars and then ride all the roads until they knew every foot and every turn in them. There must be no last-minute panic, no confusion, no mistakes. Two cars were to be on one side of the train, two on the other, and the mail thieves would ride off in opposite directions after the robbery.

The men were in a daze. Four cars! Four cars needed to carry away the mail sacks. This was robbery on a scale that none of them had ever attempted before.

Murray said that the best meeting place after the robbery, where they could distribute the loot, was a paint shop that his uncle owned at Ottawa, Illinois, which was now empty.

The time of the robbery was set for June 12. The mail train was to leave from Union Station. Two of the men, Willis Newton and Herbert Holliday, waited in the train shed until the last minute, hiding in the dark. Just as the train began to move they climbed between the tender and the first car.

The place selected for the robbery was Rondout. As they approached, the two bandits scrambled into the engineer's cab, showing that they were armed.

"Stop when you see a red light."

A red light appeared ahead and the train rolled to a stop. The three other Newton men and Glasscock were waiting. As soon as the train stopped, the mail clerks locked the doors and turned out the lights. Shots began to come through the windows. The clerks lay on the floor of the cars to escape the bullets. Then poison gas began to be pumped in. There was no chance for the clerks and they knew it. They opened the doors and stumbled out into the fresh air.

As a rule, a totally unexpected happening takes people unaware and they do not think quickly or clearly. But there was one man on the train who did not lose his wits and panic, even when he saw how many armed bandits there were. This was a brakeman named Sandy MacRae. Instead of standing with his hands high over his head, as he was ordered, he ran straight toward the armed gunmen, shouting in what seemed to be genuine terror.

"There's another train due!" he yelled. "If I can't send word through at once, there will be a wreck. You won't get anything."

The bandits let him go. MacRae raced to the nearest train phone and sent word that the train was being held up; help should be sent at once. That was the first mistake the bandits made.

At that time, however, they had no thought of mistakes. They were hauling down the loot, looking for the mail sacks which Fahy had indicated. In that haul they took $2,050,511 in cash, diamonds, negotiable securities, Liberty bonds, so tremendous an amount of money that they were almost stunned by their good luck.

No matter how well a criminal lays his plans, something is almost bound to come unstuck. So, in the confusion and the darkness, Willie Newton moved from the position in which he had been ordered to stay. Glasscock saw the moving figure and put five bullets in him. Then Willie's brother Jess found him and helped carry him to one of the getaway cars. And that was the second mistake. Because of the shooting, other investigators entered the case.

As a result of MacRae's prompt warning, men began to gather while the robbery was still going on, and before long they began to appear at the scene of the crime. First to arrive were local sheriffs, followed by men from the railroad police and the Chicago police. The last to show up was Bill Fahy, usually the first, prompt, alert, and ready to plunge into any problem at a moment's notice.

As Fahy had foreseen, there were no clues that were of any use. So many highways stretched out in all directions that there was no indication of where the men had gone. But one thing they knew. One of the bandits had been seriously wounded by those five bullets. So every doctor and hospital in the area was alerted to report any patient who had gunshot wounds.

Of course, Fahy was the man in charge, as he had anticipated. The first thing he heard must have upset him a great deal, though he gave no evidence of it. Chief Clerk Phillips told him that the bandits had known what to look for. That meant that this was an inside job. Someone from the Postal Service itself must have indicated which mail sacks were valuable.

Murray, meanwhile, had taken the wounded Willie Newton to Chicago for treatment. He called Dr. Mitchell S. Corbett and asked him to treat a man who had been accidentally shot in crossfire from a rumrunning fight.

Dr. Corbett treated the man. Later he read the newspaper where there was a long account of the spectacular train robbery. At once the doctor telephoned Captain Schoemaker of the Chicago police and reported the case of the patient with the gunshot wounds. It was possible that Murray's explanation had been a lie and that this was one of the wanted bandits.

The police captain was interested. "Where did you treat this patient?"

"At the apartment of Walter McComb." The doctor gave him the address.

Schoemaker knew that McComb was a bootlegger. He rounded up some detectives and went to the address Dr. Corbett had given him. They found not only Willie, who was a very sick man indeed, but his brother Joe Newton as well.

Indignantly the two men insisted that their name was Wade. They had never heard of these Newtons. The detectives searched the men and the rooms carefully and turned up two new Federal Reserve bank notes, one for $500 and the other for $1,000.

"How did you get these?"

The Newtons had no answer.

Schoemaker sent Willie to the county jail hospital and Joe was put in the jail. The McComb apartment was to be watched, both from inside and from the street.

About two in the morning there was a cautious knock at the door. In came Murray, who was horrified to find not the members of his gang but members of the police.

Schoemaker noticed bloodstains on Murray's clothes. "How did you get these?"

In the darkness and the excitement Murray had not noticed them and he could think of no convincing explanation. But he had had experience with Fahy, so he assumed other law-enforcement officers were equally corrupt. He tried to bribe

Schoemaker to forget he had seen him. It didn't work.

At three o'clock in the morning Willis Newton came to the apartment. The gang was falling easily into the arms of the waiting police.

A short time later Captain Schoemaker telephoned Fahy to tell him that four of the gang had been caught, identified, and were under arrest. For the rest of that night Fahy must have had bitter thoughts. Everything had gone wrong. There should have been no clues to the identity of the gang, no shooting, no involvement with the Chicago police or any other law-enforcement agency. The investigation ought to have been left entirely to him. Now, because of blunders and accidents, there were other men working at the solution of the crime; it was no longer his to handle in his own way. Sooner or later the other Postal Inspectors were bound to notice that he wasn't getting anywhere.

Next day the prisoners were brought up for questioning. Fahy, of course, asked the questions, but Schoemaker was on hand, and there were other inspectors looking on. Things had certainly gone wrong.

One thing, however, was still going right. The prisoners looked at Fahy without recognition. They could not give him away. In his hands rested their only chance of getting off lightly.

So far Jess Newton, Holliday, and Glasscock, who had mistakenly shot Willie, were still free. They knew the others had been caught and that they were under heavy bail. Murray was able to put up a bond of $50,000, was freed, and promptly disappeared.

At their hide-out the free men counted their loot, divided it, and buried most of it. It was important that they should not be seen together, as their freedom and the use of all the money depended on not being recognized. Glasscock set off for Chicago, taking along $8,000 in cash and $100,000 in Liberty bonds, which Murray was to share with Fahy, promising that there would be a great deal more. The rest would come as soon as it was safe to bring it out into circulation.

Fahy was acting oddly. Because of his past reputation he was greatly respected, but this time he wasn't confiding in anyone; he wasn't trying to keep the other Postal Inspectors informed of the course of his investigation. That was queer. They set it down to the fact that, unlikely as it appeared, he was trying to solve the case alone and get all the credit.

Certainly he appeared to be working hard. Every day he looked more tired and strained. But still the case wasn't getting anywhere. Fahy hadn't cleared up a single point. It was Captain Schoemaker who had brought in part of the gang. It was other Postal Inspectors now who began to turn up information. They found pictures of the missing men: Jess Newton, Brent Glasscock, and Herbert Holliday. They got an identification of the pictures from mail clerks who had been on the robbed train. They distributed WANTED circulars on the bandits, with a reward of $2,000, dead or alive.

And still Fahy remained strangely inactive. The other Postal Inspectors carried on by themselves. The circulars began to pay off. They turned up Herbert Holliday in Little Rock, Arkansas. Then the inspectors heard that Jess Newton had gone to Mexico. How were they to lure him back across the border? They recalled that Jess claimed that he was a great rider, so they sent into Mexico placards advertising a rodeo show with a prize for the best rider. Jess fell for it and came rushing back to take part. He was picked up at the border.

There was now only one member of the gang who had never shown up. This was Glasscock. Then the police got an excited telephone call from the owner of a boardinghouse in Battle Creek, Michigan. A new boarder had just come and he looked like the picture of the missing man.

Dozens of people make such calls, of course, about any wanted man; they are always followed up. This time the tip was a sound one. They found Glasscock, and in his suitcase they turned up $80,000.

The Postal Inspectors had now discovered all the members of the gang. The time had come for them to talk. And they did. They described the crime, told about the accidental shooting, the stolen getaway cars, the hide-out, the distribution of the loot, their final attempts to get as far away as they could from the hide-out and from each other.

"But this," the Postal Inspectors insisted, "must have been an inside crime. Who told you about the mail train and which mail sacks were valuable?"

The members of the gang shook their heads blankly. There hadn't been any such person. And Fahy continued with the questions that didn't seem to get anywhere, that did not help clear up the crime. In fact, when Willie Newton was first identified by a mail clerk as the man who had been shot, Fahy appeared not to believe him; he set to work deliberately to break down the man's testimony.

It was then that an ugly suspicion struck the Postal Service. For the first time it seemed possible that one of their own men was disloyal to the service, dishonest in his dealings. They did not want to believe it. Fahy had a splendid record and they were proud of him. At thirty-five he was one of the most promising men in the whole department. Perhaps he had been overworking.

When the whole gang was arrested, Fahy did not share in the jubilation of the other Postal Inspectors. He seemed to brood, to grow more gloomy every day. Then more disturbing rumors reached the anxious Postal Inspectors. The superintendent of a postal station reported that a policeman had commented to him that Fahy had been seen around some very expensive places and that he was drinking a lot.

Finally Willie Bush, of the main post office in Chicago, went to Washington to see the Chief Inspector. Bush knew Fahy well and had worked with him in the past. But what he had come to report was that one day he had entered Fahy's Chicago office unexpectedly and found him talking with Murray who was the major link with the mail thieves.

Grimly the men in the service determined to root out the one dishonor of their history. Bush called on Fahy and told him that he had heard the Washington Bureau was sending another man to Chicago to look into the mail robbery. At once Fahy put in a telephone call to the Ambassador Hotel and asked for Mr. C. Anderson. Mr. C. Anderson answered in the voice of Murray and Fahy repeated the warning. He told Murray to stay in the hotel. No telling who the new man might be or what he might be up to.

So Fahy was arrested by his fellow Postal Inspectors. No other man had ever failed to uphold the splendid standards of the Department.

By law the verdict was twenty-five years to be served in the federal prison at Atlanta for the armed robbery of the mail. Fahy received that terrible verdict with bowed head. Worse even than his failure to master-mind a crime, worse than his loss of an easy fortune, worse than the fact that the rest of his active life would be spent behind bars, was the open shame and contempt of the men with whom he had worked for so long.

With Fahy and the bandits shut away the Postal Inspectors carried on, and in the end they had either recovered or been able to account for all but a little over $20,000 of the proceeds of the great train robbery.

XIV ☆ Violence Airborne

VIOLENCE HAS TAKEN various forms during the years, so the laboratories are trained today in the dangerous business of dismantling or making a bomb harmless. In the past it was thought that dropping a bomb in water would do the trick. But bombs, like everything else, are now made of new materials, and if calcium phosphide is used it may create a gas when it is dropped in water, which will explode it. Today it is usual to soak the bomb in oil.

Use of bombs sent by mail became a frequent occurrence in Chicago at the time when the Mafia, or the Black Hand, began to terrorize the Italian immigrants there. The Black Hand letters, with their skull and crossbones insignia, paralyzed their victims with fear. If they did not turn over the money demanded of them by these extortion letters, they were sometimes tortured; often their homes were bombed.

Because the victims were afraid of the Mafia, they did not want to reveal the names of the people who were causing all this violence. Too many people, even today, abjectly obey the orders of dictators, believing that it is easier to surrender than to exert a little courage.

In time a few of the poor victims came to realize that the

138

Postal Inspection Service represented a greater force of security than they got by simply doing what the Black Hand people told them to do. In 1919 the Mafia gang was arrested, one hundred witnesses were persuaded to testify against them, and they went to prison.

Down in the South a man received a parcel-post package and opened it while he was sitting in his car with his bride of a few months. The package contained a bomb that exploded, killing the man outright and gravely injuring his wife.

Postal Inspectors from Washington were assigned to the case. They were J. E. Santner, B. B. Webb, and C. H. Burrows. There was no difficulty in establishing the identity of victim, who was a man named Curry Thomas. According to the postmaster at Cape Charles, the parcel had had a return address: C. F. Thomas, Richmond, Virginia.

There was no C. F. Thomas in Richmond, so the Postal Inspectors went over the wrecked car and then began to study the entire scene of the crime. To begin with, there didn't seem to be any clues, but they gathered up everything they found: little bits of wire, a torn fragment of paper marked " 'dis C battery" and "atteries, Inc." There were also small pieces of steel pipe and iron caps.

This was all that could be found. Yet these tiny and apparently meaningless scraps of clues were to provide leads that pin-pointed the murderer.

The piece of wire was from a mousetrap, so they assumed a lid-mousetrap type of bomb. Because the tiny pieces of metal were no bigger than shrapnel they were sure that the bomb contained dynamite, which, when exploded inside a sealed pipe, causes an equal pressure all along the pipe.

They examined the other small fragments. A piece of pasteboard indicated that the bomb had been mailed in a corrugated carton, probably tied with string.

One of the most difficult problems in committing the crime of murder is to conceal the identity of the victim. Once this is established, it becomes, as a rule, comparatively easy to discover the criminal. Detective stories to the contrary, there are rarely a number of people who want to kill a certain individual.

The victim's wife was in a hospital, seriously ill from her injuries. She could tell the Postal Inspectors nothing about any reason for her husband's murder. She knew of no one who disliked him. She could, however, describe the package, so she gave them a clear account of its approximate size, its appearance, how it was wrapped, addressed, and stamped. With this information the Postal Inspectors made up a dummy parcel, which they showed to postmasters, hoping that one would remember having handled such a parcel.

Meantime the Postal Inspectors, trained to be alert at analyzing the people whom they are questioning, felt that Mrs. Thomas had been too emphatic in saying that no one disliked her husband; they suspected that she was withholding vital information. They began to look into her background and learned that she had worked before her marriage as a receptionist for a dentist.

They went to see the dentist, who was shocked by the fatal accident but had no information to give them about his former receptionist. Delving deeper, the inspectors looked up Mrs. Thomas's former associates, her business acquaintances, personal friends, and members of her family.

One of the young women whom she had known well said that the dentist had been in love with Mrs. Thomas and that he had been greatly upset over her marriage to another man.

Here was a motive for the crime. Again the Postal Inspectors questioned the dentist, but he had a perfect alibi for the day when the bomb had been mailed in Richmond. He had been on a fishing trip with a friend of his, two hundred and fifty miles away.

The friend backed up the alibi. It was quite true, he assured them. For two days he and the dentist had been fishing. Ordinarily this would have been a sound confirmation of the alibi, but in this case the Postal Inspectors were not satisfied. The friend's account of that fishing trip was almost word for word the same as the dentist's. People don't talk alike as a rule; they don't express things in the same way; they don't stress the same things as important. When they do, it seems most probable that they have agreed on the story in advance.

While they were looking into the background of the unfortunate Mr. Thomas and his stricken wife, the Postal Inspectors followed up all the tiny clues they had gathered near the wrecked car. Easiest to check was the label from the battery. A Cleveland firm said it was from a dry-cell radio battery, sold to hardware stores exclusively. Knowing the general vicinity of the crime, the Postal Inspectors began that long, patient checking of theirs. They got records from the Cleveland firm, showing that a sale of this kind of battery had been made to a store in the same building where the dentist had his office.

The inspectors talked to the clerk in the hardware store. He had sold the dentist not only a dry-cell battery but also some dynamite, which his brother needed on his farm.

A firm in Auburn, New York, identified the fragment of twine as its own manufacture. They had sold the identical brand to dealers who finally turned up in their records a shipment of supplies they had made to the dentist, tied up with the twine. To make things easier for them—and things aren't often made easier for the inspectors—this dentist was their only customer in that area.

They had accounted for the battery, the dynamite, even the twine on the package. They knew what kind of bomb it had been, because of the wire from the mousetrap. Now they began to search for the steel pipe, for the pieces of iron that they had found in shattered fragments beside the car. A plumbing company was uncertain at first. Then a clerk remembered that two steel nipples, two pieces of iron pipe five inches long, and four iron caps for the pipe had been bought not long before by this same dentist.

By this time the evidence seemed to be overwhelming. But there was still one major factor. They had no proof that he had mailed the package. With the dummy that had been reconstructed from Mrs. Thomas's description, the inspectors began to make the rounds of all post office branches. In a dry-goods store, where there was a local branch, a mail clerk said, "I remember that package."

"What makes you remember it?"

"Well, I was struck by the fact that the names of the sender and of the receiver were the same. It just stuck in my mind for some reason."

"Do you know who mailed this?"

"Not by name." But the clerk had a good visual memory and he described the dentist.

Back the Postal Inspectors went to see the fishing companion to try to crack that alibi. Why, of course, they had been together, he assured them easily. The inspectors asked whether he knew that the dentist was facing a murder charge and that, as his accomplice in providing an alibi, he was to be arrested.

In horror the friend admitted that the story was a fake from beginning to end. But the dentist had told him that the whole thing was a practical joke. He had had no idea that the dentist had performed a cold-blooded murder.

In 1957 President Eisenhower signed a bill providing the death penalty or life imprisonment for killing by mail. The reason for this was the most spectacular tragedy to result from airborne violence.

This law came about because of the great airplane disaster that had occurred two years earlier, when a four-engined commercial airliner exploded over Longmont, Colorado. That explosion cost the lives of more than forty innocent persons.

Because the airliner carried mail, Postal Inspectors were at once ordered to the scene to protect it. When necessary, indeed, these men have to salvage mail in such disasters as plane and train wrecks, fires, and floods. In the case of a plane accident, men from a number of investigative groups co-operate to solve the case, each group of men operating within the field of his special knowledge and responsibility.

All the vast machinery that protects the mail was set to work, operating swiftly and surely. The mail clerk at the Denver Air Mail Field was asked to get a copy of the mail manifest and a description of the registered mail that had been put on the plane at Denver. The Acting Regional Transportation Manager was to be picked up at the loading dock of the Denver Post Office. At the same time Inspector Carl H. Pollock was ordered to get to the scene of the disaster as fast as he could and see that the mail was not stolen or tampered with. Two other Postal Inspectors were to pick up a third, meet United Airlines officials, and reach the airliner without wasting a minute. One of the inspectors described the operations as follows:

"Inspector John A. McCullough had been alerted and I picked him up en route to the post office. At the dock we loaded empty sacks into the car and then headed north.

"It was the third time some of us had made the trip north on Highway 87 on just such a mission . . .

"We joined Inspectors Windbigler, Murphy, and Cooper at the rendezvous point just as the United Air Lines rescue bus was ready to depart. We could see the reddish yellow glow of twin fires some miles to the northeast across the fields. A pilot car led the way and we turned off the dirt road into a farmyard and followed along the edge of the plowed field until progress was barred by a deep ditch.

"The growing convoy turned west along the ditch and across the field. A helicopter milled in from the south and zigzagged across the area, coming down low and dropping flares. The flares lit up a wide path of debris with fragments of the metal skin of the plane, seats, personal effects, and crumpled bodies.

"Detouring around deep irrigation ditches and fences, we were able to drive our cars as close to the wreckage as prudence indicated . . .

"A short-wave set was in use. The Colorado State Highway Patrol had called in all cars and men from nearby counties and placed road blocks around the area in which it was known that debris had fallen. Other prowl cars cruised the perimeter to keep out the morbidly curious.

"Our crew was joined by representatives of the Railway Express Agency on a like mission. We had not seen any mail in the debris as we drove across the fields, but in the pale moonlight we could follow the path of debris to the south and slightly west. We formed a skirmish line with wide intervals between men, and zigzagged across the field as we worked south.

". . . no mail until we reached the south boundary line and then only scattered pieces. A Civilian Defense car came by with a report that there was considerable mail at the point where the tail of the plane had come to rest, some two miles south of the place where the body of the plane crashed . . .

"The tail . . . rested upright . . . and had come to earth so gently that it had not furrowed the plowed ground. Several distinctive orange-colored mail sacks were recovered, all of them badly torn. Some letters, still tied in bundles, were cut or shredded as though they had been thrown or dragged at terrific speed across the ragged edges of the metal skin of the shattered plane.

"The mail recovered there showed no evidence of fire or of being subjected to intense heat.

"We paused after we had gathered up the mail. It must have been close to midnight. A freezing wind blew from the high mountains across the barren fields. No one had much to say as we sipped hot coffee from our thermos jugs, but I think it was about this time that we concluded that we were probably confronted by maniacal mass murder, and faced the possibility that the murderer had used the air mails to accomplish his fiendish objective."

There were a number of reasons for coming to this conclusion. The disaster had not been caused by fire or by the blowing up of an engine. There were some characteristic signs about the explosion that had destroyed the plane. One thing the investigators were sure of. The explosion had been caused by dynamite. But where and how had the dynamite been carried: in the passenger compartment, in the luggage of one of the passengers, or in the mailbags?

It was, of course, the mailbags that most concerned the Postal Inspectors. They examined all the mail they found, sniffing at it for the smell of dynamite. Somehow or other they had to find every piece that remained.

"We drove south," Inspector in Charge Dunbar reported, "parked, and climbed a barbwire fence in the marshy meadows west of the county road. Spreading out, we did find considerable mail scattered along a north-south pattern and extending nearly a mile.

"The area we were covering was becoming wider and we worked well apart, each man going on as his findings warranted. Where the meadows had been flooded, the half-frozen places could not bear our weight, and the chill of the wind was accentuated by wet feet."

Nonetheless they recovered about a hundred pounds of mail and processed it for forwarding. By that time it was three o'clock on a cold and dark morning. A great pit had been dug by the nose of the plane as it fell and here they found another two hundred pounds of mail.

The Postal Inspectors had done their job; it was time now

for the Federal Bureau of Investigation to carry on with other aspects, as it was apparent that the dynamite had not been in the mailbags.

The FBI investigators learned at the airport that the plane had been twelve minutes late in taking off because one of the passengers had been delayed. If the plane had left on schedule, that explosion would have occurred over the Rockies and no clues would ever have been found as to the cause of the disaster.

Carefully the investigators went over the list of passengers, checking on all of them. One case stood out and caught their attention. A Mrs. Daisy King had discovered at the last minute that her luggage was overweight, though she had arranged to have it the proper weight. Her son by a former marriage, John Gilbert Graham, had persuaded her that she would need all of it.

John Gilbert Graham had, the FBI men learned, taken out $38,500 flight insurance on his mother's life before she boarded the plane. Now they were really interested. Gilbert was not unknown to the law. His mother, wealthy by reason of her third husband's fortune, had tried her best to help her son to help himself, investing heavily in a small business for him, but the shop she had purchased for him was blown up. It had been heavily insured and the insurance people paid because they could find no substantial evidence against Graham. The young man also had a record of forgery.

Little by little, evidence of the crime that cost more than forty lives was emerging. Someone had heard Graham say, "I'd do anything for money." His wife testified that they had stopped at the airport for a drink after the plane left but that Graham had been too sick to finish his drink. When they got home he had turned on the radio, heard the news of the explosion, and had collapsed completely.

By the next morning, however, Graham seems to have recovered completely from his shock and his sense of guilt. He saw no reason to do an extra day's work as long as he had so much money coming to him, so he quit his job.

By routine investigation the FBI learned that Graham had got hold of twenty-five sticks of dynamite with a timing device and an electric battery, which he had placed in his mother's luggage at the last moment before the plane left.

Arrested by the FBI and confronted with the overwhelming evidence against him, Graham confessed to the crime and was given a death sentence.

CONCLUSION

XV ☆ The Postal Inspectors
and the Public

FROM THE TIME when the United States Government began
to function we have had a small and devoted group of men
whose job it has been to protect the mails from theft, from
fraud, from violence. They have had an even harder job than
that, trying to protect the American people from their own
gullibility. They have tried to save them from fake medical
advice and dishonest claims.

They have succeeded magnificently. Their record, as an
investigative group and as individuals, reflects honor on us
as well as on them. They have proved over and over that
only a very stupid criminal will risk tangling with Uncle
Sam, because the Postal Inspectors never give up and, in
the long run, they get their man. Of course, they can't always
protect people from themselves, but as time goes on they hope
that more and more enlightened citizens will develop more
sturdy sense:

a) That they won't invest money without knowing that
they are dealing with a genuine organization;

b) That they won't fall for "get-rich-quick" schemes,

which enrich only the chiselers;

c) That they won't fall for fairy tales about something for nothing;

d) That they will not risk their health, sometimes even their lives, by using "cures" that are not recommended by reputable physicians;

e) That they will report at once to their local postmaster the receipt of anonymous or threatening letters of any kind that may come into their hands;

f) That they will turn over to their postmaster any mail that is pornographic or obscene in character;

g) That they inform their postmaster at once of the receipt of any mail containing Communist propaganda, so that its source may be immediately determined and dealt with.

The Postal Inspectors do all they can, but no group of public servants, however efficient and honorable and incorruptible they may be, can do the job alone. They need the support and the co-operation of the public.

We all owe them something, from the most obscure citizen to the President himself. Indeed, the late President Kennedy himself may well have been saved from assassination three years before he was actually killed by an assassin's bullet. A vigilant Postal Inspector in New Hampshire found that a local individual had threatened to murder the newly elected President and had headed for Palm Beach. The alert Inspector got in touch with the secret service men who guard the President. The latter found the would-be assassin and promptly arrested him.

At this very moment Postal Inspectors are hard at work, checking misleading advertisements, studying the efficient operation of a post office, tracking down a mail thief, following a criminal, making a dreary stake-out or risking their lives in fire or flood or hurricane, so that the United States mail may go peacefully, safely, and quickly on its way.

INDEX

Index

157